MIRROR

True Stories of Unusual Rides and Crazy Passengers
From a Late-Night Uber Driver

BRIAN DIXON
"THE DRIVINGFOOL"

First Edition
Brian Dixon
" The Driving Fool"

REARVIEW MIRROR

True Stories of Unusual Rides and Crazy Passengers
From a Late-Night Uber Driver

BRIAN DIXON

"THE DRIVINGFOOL"

COPYRIGHT

To Melaina, a beautiful but troubled young lady I unfortunately will never have the pleasure of meeting. And to Carlos, Melaina's father, whom I had the privilege to meet at a very inopportune time. Thank you for reminding me how precious life is, how short it can sometimes be, and how important your loved ones are. May you and your family heal and eventually find some peace.

CONTENTS

INTRODUCTION

I magine getting into your car every evening and driving strangers from place to place until the early morning hours. Having been a "transportation professional" in the Silicon Valley region of the San Francisco Bay Area for five years and 21,337 logged trips, I spent many hours looking in my rearview mirror at the person sitting in the back of my car. Driving could sometimes be an unpredictable experience, but it was rarely a dull one.

I didn't plan on being a rideshare driver, but fell into the personal rideshare business due to unplanned circumstances. Initially, I took the job to generate income while I worked on a slow-moving startup with some partners. However, the new venture took longer than expected, and I found myself liking the anonymity of driving and setting my own hours. Plus, there was never a shortage of drama and I rarely had an uneventful night.

Ridesharing was an unconventional job, like no other I had ever experienced. Driving was the easy part, despite Bay Area traffic. Interacting with the many different passengers was more challenging, and it was also what made the job interesting.

There were many fascinating people that crossed my path, and a few I wished hadn't. I drove serial startup entrepreneurs, powerful venture capitalists, and starry-eyed, over-optimistic new founders looking to launch their first company. Combine this with the desperate, lost, and street-savvy crowd and it added up to a very interesting, but volatile, cocktail of humanity. All were a fascinating mix of sociology and psychology.

I gave rides to professional athletes, sports announcers, and a handful of multi-millionaires in t-shirts and jeans—young engineers or technology managers who spoke their own unique dialects and whose conversations sounded like a foreign language. I once had a pooled ride with four separate passengers, each from a different country. It was a dynamic conversation, to say the least.

I took four people to the emergency room: a tech employee, a mother who was having an allergic reaction, a teen with a cut hand, and a woman who had such a bad case of the flu, I thought she was going to pass out in my car.

My vomit record was pretty good, as I only had one incident inside my car in five years. Unfortunately, the passenger had eaten curry earlier that evening.

Much to my chagrin, I have been propositioned multiple times, from both sexes. I am not saying this to boast, only that it's an occupational hazard. I have seen two sets of bare breasts, both unrequested displays. Alcohol was obviously involved. It didn't suck.

I gave a ride to a *Sister of Perpetual Indulgence* coming from a show in the Castro District of San Francisco. Decked out in full drag, she complained, "Darling, my feet are on fire because of these damn heels. I can't wait to get home to a nice glass of wine and my cat." You have to love The City.

Passengers have smoked crack in my back seat. A "meth head" went into a screaming tirade about his recent incarceration and pounded on my dash. I have also been the transport vehicle for a drug deal, unbeknownst to me, until the passenger got back into the car with a wad of cash. No injuries were sustained in any of these incidents.

I once picked up the same guy four times in 20 minutes. He was on a project deadline for work, needed to make copies, and forgot something essential each time I dropped him off. When I dropped him off for the last time, I laughingly told him I didn't wasn't to see him again for a month!

A prostitute solicited business from my back seat as we passed a potential prospect. I indulged her, stopped the car, and the two chatted for a few minutes. In the end, he declined the offer. She thanked me after the ride and tipped me well.

I gave a very drunk young woman a ride home late one weekend night. She was "touch-and-go" for the majority of the trip, and I was speeding to avoid an accident in my back seat. As soon as the car stopped, she flung herself out of my car and threw up all over the side of my Prius. I rolled my window down, and heard her mumble, "I think I got a little on your car," as she took off her jacket off and started wiping the chunky mess all over my vehicle.

If I had a dime for every drunk person that used me as a cheap therapist, I could comfortably retire.

Items left in my car included sunglasses, headphones, cell phones, makeup, keys, fries, pens, glitter, scarves, superglue, a receipt for a recently purchased $2,400 TAG Heuer watch, water bottles, hats, a can of unopened beer, shoes, red solo cups with alcohol, toothpicks, and more iPhone cords than I could count. I have been offered various drugs by multiple passengers. One enthusiastic "stoner" gave me an oversized bag of pot, even though I told him I didn't smoke. I gave it to a friend who does, in exchange for pizza and beer. My friend happened to be on vacation for a week, so I kept the bag in my room, which made it smell like a dispensary. Everybody was happy in the end.

My in-the-car burrito consumption over five years easily exceeded 800—that's an average of three to four burritos a week. A special shout-out goes out to Pancho Villa Taqueria, Super Tacos el Conrad, and Tacos Santiaguito. All were culinary lifesavers when the late-night munchies hit. If I needed a great slice, there was no other choice than Bibo's NY Pizza.

Two different couples broke up in my car. I have slept in my car more times than I can count, and stopped an ongoing ride three times, kicking out abusive and/or aggressive passengers. I also had to warn a couple to stop with their amorous display of affection, for fear the situation would escalate. They grumbled but complied.

The situations I found myself in, as a driver, were as contrasting as the riders who got into my car. I never really knew what was coming next. Fortunately, I liked a dose of unpredictability now and again, so the job fed that craving nicely.

What follows is a collection of some of my favorite and memorable stories from the road. I tried to capture a front-seat view of what it's like to drive full-time in this wild profession. I've also included some of my personal insights into the driving industry, along with a few tips on driver and passenger etiquette based on my years of experience.

When this literary journey started, my intent was to simply share my experiences, and give readers a taste of the driving business. As more words hit the page, a second motive developed: empathy. In addition to sharing some good fun and a few wild rides, I sincerely hope you gain a better appreciation for the over 5.5 million drivers worldwide. All are looking to give you a safe, friendly, and reasonably-priced ride. Drivers do their best to get their customers where they need to go. Be kind to them, the job isn't always as easy as it seems.

Note: All stories are true, with a few minor details left out where appropriate. Names have been changed to protect the innocent and the not-so innocent.

JUST PLAIN FUN

Ask a hundred rideshare drivers what the best part of their driving day was, and invariably, ninety-nine will say their passengers.

Laughter comes easily to me, so I naturally connected with those riders who had a sense of humor. If they had an outgoing personality, even better. I purposely shifted the conversation to encourage their antics.

Passengers who had been drinking, especially if they had a comedic streak, told jokes about that night's adventures, their partners, their families, and even their bosses. Some had me in stitches to the point that I could barely drive. I was a neutral entity, and because they would never see me again, they felt comedic freedom without limitations.

Kids were especially amusing, as they spoke the truth without a filter. This form of pure expression meant you never knew what would come next. Some of my best conversations were with youngsters.

If I was fortunate to get a few funny passengers in my car, it would set the tone for the rest of the evening.

♫
SWEET MUSIC TO MY EARS

*"Now look lady, you may have heard a lot of singers
but you ain't heard nothin' sung till you've heard me sung it."
-Dino, Kiss Me, Stupid*

Many of my younger passengers asked me to turn on music when they got in my car. Here in San Jose, this often translates to hip-hop. Some are content with the radio, others prefer to listen to their own tunes. However, most middle-age passengers prefer conversation over music. On a warm Saturday night in June, a couple in their 50s would prove that theory wrong and show that they had some rhythm too.

I am a musicophile; I enjoy various kinds of music including blues, classic rock, Motown, indie, and occasionally even country. Foo Fighters one day, Ray Charles the next. Current hip-hop has never been my go-to genre. I can do some of the old-school stuff like Run DMC, the Beastie Boys, Outkast and Eminem. But today, the style of hip-hop is the variable. Whether it's the G-funk groove for the young Latin girls, pop-rap for the teens, or edgy gangsta rap for the angry white boys, hip-hop transcends age and color.

Despite my aversion to modern hip-hop, the music makes sense. In a lot of ways, it represents the same ideals rock and roll did for my age group—it's the voice of the younger generation. A vehicle for commentary about current society, and a tool to give voice to the frustration over social issues that need to change. Hip-hop is also the polar opposite of voice-synthesized pop music, and I say amen to that. In the end, it's also about sex and money, a trait it shares with good-old rock and roll.

One might compare the current hip-hop craze to the punk scene in the 1970s, except this genre is not simply a musical period in time, it is evolving. Many successful rappers have gone on to start multi-million record labels, act, produce, and create musical empires: 50 Cent, Ice Cube, Dr. Dre and LL Cool J. So, while I appreciate the genre, in the end, I'm an old white guy; I don't have as much angst as I used to.

Two passengers, Don and Francine, a couple close to me in age, had a touch of rebellion and a handful of gusto about them. They were partying on Santana Row, an upscale collaboration of high-end lofts, expensive retail, and a movie theater. Due to the infusion of tech startups in the area, it's grown into a luxury community, with no shortage of good restaurants and popular bars. You can even buy a Tesla, as the luxury car manufacturer has a retail showroom there. It is a destination spot for wealthy tourists, locals looking for a fun night, and out-of-town visitors seeking one of San Jose's better nighttime areas.

The strip gets maddeningly crowded on the weekends. Massive crowds fill the streets, making turns in your car a lesson in patience. As any rideshare driver will attest, this area is prime picking grounds if you are in need of a new passenger.

Ordinarily, older couples tend to be more subdued, closing out most evenings between 10:00 p.m. and 11:00 p.m., ready for a rational night's sleep. After a big meal, a couple of drinks, the pillow calls their name. However, Don and Francine were far from your typical subdued couple. For starters, they burst into my car with a shot of enthusiasm.

"Hey Brian, how's it going?" Don started the conversation in a deafening tone that startled me.

New passengers often greet drivers like they have known them for years, after getting their first names from the app on their phone. It's not impersonal, and it doesn't bother me, having learned to appreciate the effort. I really enjoy friendly riders like this, as they make trips seem shorter and far more tolerable.

I was in an amiable mood, and fired back at them with the same energy, "Great kids, how are *you* doing?"

"We're awesome!" Don bellowed back. I sensed this would be an interesting ride.

Don was a big man, assertive in an easygoing way, completing his jovial look with a full grey beard. Francine was tall and lean, with a quick smile and infectious laugh. Both were gregarious, likable, and super cute together.

It was obvious they'd had a few glasses of wine at dinner and were feeling no pain, but they hadn't overindulged. The perfect passengers in my mind—happy but not sloppy.

Without prompting, Francine chimed in, "We're in town from Phoenix. Don has clients to see. We thought we would make a weekend of it here in the Bay Area."

"That sounds fun," I obliged. "Welcome."

"Thanks, do you have any tunes in this car?" she asked, obviously wanting to continue her good mood.

My radio has two preset levels. The first set is for my passengers, and has a variety of musical genres. The other is for my personal use and consists of rock, indie and NPR.

"Of course," I replied and started to go through the list of stations. Starting with the pop stations, I quickly moved to the indie channel, then a bit of R&B, waiting for an emphatic confirmation.

"Come on, don't you have any old school rock?" Don asked with a bit of impatience. The way he said it made it clear there was no other kind of music people could possibly want to listen to.

"Gotcha covered," I laughed, quickly switched to my stations, and hit the first of six preset channels. It would take me a few tries to hit solid gold.

Pushing my first rock button, Metallica's *Enter Sandman* came on, as James Hetfield growled *Off to Never Neverland* through my speakers. Definitely too hard, I thought, and kept moving. Francine concurred. On the next channel, the soaring voice of Steve Perry of Journey serenaded us with *Don't Stop Believing*. Francine seemed to like this one, but Don quickly jumped in with his two cents, "Good song but a little too mellow."

I saw that these people were serious about their music choices. On the last attempt, one of AC/DC's recognizable anthems struck a nerve:

> *Cause the walls were shaking*
> *The earth was quaking*
> *My mind was aching*
> *And we were making it and you*
> *Shook me all night long*
> *Yeah you shook me all night long*

"That's the ticket!" Don screamed and began singing along.

Now, when I say singing, I don't mean at a level slightly above a speaking voice. I mean he was belting it out at full capacity. I secretly loved his unbridled enthusiasm. It didn't take Francine more than two seconds to catch the fever, and she joined in as loudly as she could.

Don paused the duet momentarily and asked, "Do you know this one Brian?"

Now, I have listened to AC/DC since high school, when Bon Scott, before his untimely death, was the band's front man. Their 1979 album, *Highway to Hell*, is, in my humble opinion, one of the greatest rock albums ever recorded.

"Come on, I grew up with AC/DC!" I barked back, obviously caught up in the mayhem.

Don hit my shoulder in an encouraging thump, and yelled, "Then sing, Brian, sing!"

Francine immediately nodded and doubled up on the pressure. "Yeah, sing with us!"

Well...what would you do? Realistically, it wasn't really a request, and I was more than happy to oblige. We cruised down the 17-South Freeway, hit Highway 85 toward Almaden Valley, windows down, the volume high, and sang in unison:

> *You really took me and you*
> *Shook me all night long*
> *You shook me all night long*
> *Yeah, yeah, you shook me all night long*
> *You really got me and you*
> *Shook me all night long*
> *Yeah you shook me*
> *Yeah you shook me*
> *All night long*

Like I said, I'm an old white guy. I may not have as much angst as I used to, but a dose of good old rock and roll still moves me.

There we were, three geezers, reliving our high school party days and having a grand time. It made me realize that life is what you make it. You're either a wallflower or a participant. I choose the latter.

Thanks for the reminder, Don and Francine. Keep rocking and singing till the music stops!

TROUBLE WITH THE PRINCIPAL

"If you were my brother, I'd put you up for adoption."
-Amy Szalinski, Honey I Shrunk the Kids

"Hey there," I said, greeting the young student as she got into the car.

"Hi back," she answered cheerfully.

"Just finished classes?" I asked, trying to see if a conversation interested her.

"Yes, and I'm late," she said. "But don't rush, the kids will have a project keeping them busy."

It was 5:00 p.m., rush hour. Glancing at my Uber app, the destination showed Los Altos, and despite only a ten-mile distance we were looking at a 28-minute ride.

I laughed. "Not much chance of that," I said, in case she wasn't familiar with the horrid Bay Area traffic.

Sarah was a sophomore at Mission College in Santa Clara. I found out she not only knew about the traffic, she had taken this same route hundreds of times.

"Yes, I know. I meant to get out of class earlier, but the damn teacher started talking about the rest of the semester," she said in a frustrated but accepting tone. "It's this way every year. The teachers give us a syllabus well ahead of time, both online and written, but feel compelled to go over it line by line."

"This is college, not high school, right?" I joked.

"No kidding. Guess the teachers don't think we know how to read," she said laughing.

"So, where we headed in Los Altos?" I inquired.

"Pinewood School. Do you know it?"

Los Altos is an affluent community located between Mountain View and Palo Alto, an area locals call "The Peninsula." This neighborhood is in the heart of Silicon Valley, and technology companies are the dominant occupants. Pinewood School is one of the top-rated private lower schools in Northern California. With only 120 students in grades K-2 it has a student-teacher ratio of only 6 to 1. Sending one child here will set you back a mere $33,920 annually.

"Yes, I've been to it several times," I replied. "If you don't mind me asking, you seem a little young to have kids in grade school." I was being facetious, but wanted to hear her story.

"Oh my God, no way," she laughed. "The kids are not mine. I'm their nanny. In fact, I have been with this same family since I was seventeen."

"That's nice," I replied. "I bet you have a great relationship with them."

"I do, they're practically my own kids at this stage," she said jokingly. "They are sweet kids, but the boy is a handful."

"Boys usually are," I offered.

In the brief trip to the school, I could tell Sarah was mature beyond her years—intelligent, caring and patient. She had a calming demeanor, an asset necessary for success with grade schoolers.

We arrived at the school, and I asked her if she wanted me to wait while she gathered the kids.

"No thanks. I'm not sure if they'll be ready, and I don't want to keep you waiting," she answered thoughtfully.

"Okay, have a great night," I said.

"You too," she replied.

After dropping Sarah off, I parked a few blocks away to answer a few urgent emails. I have a small "silver" fitness business on the side, training a few older clients. Absorbed in my correspondence, my Uber app rang and startled me ten minutes later.

Low and behold, a pickup at the Pinewood School.

As I pulled up to the school curb, wedged between a Tesla and a Ferrari, Sarah was standing waving at me. This time she was with a gregarious, outgoing boy of five and his enthusiastic seven-year-old sister. I love kids. I greeted them warmly and they immediately engaged me.

"Hi kids!" I said as enthusiastically as I could.

"Hello," the girl replied.

"Wassup," the boy said flippantly.

I laughed and knew this would be an interesting few minutes to their house.

"Hi Sarah," I said matter-of-factly.

"Hi Brian," she responded.

Immediately, the boy jumped into the mix. "How do you know his name?"

"Brian brought me over to your school," Sarah told him.

"No way," the boy said.

"Yes, I did," I told him.

"That's cool!" he said with gusto.

"What are your names?" I inquired.

"I'm Connor," the boy said proudly, interrupting his sister.

"I'm Haley," the seven-year old said.

"How old are you two?" I asked to get them talking, although they didn't need much prompting.

At exactly the same time, the two kids replied.

"Seven," Haley said.

"100!" Conner yelled. He corrected himself and said, "No, 200!"
"That's pretty old," I said, trying to keep from laughing out loud.

I told them I had a grandmother who was 102 years old (this was true).

The girl said, "I'm going to live to be 200!"

"Good for you," I replied.

Sarah entered the conversation and asked, "What did you do in school today?"

"I spent the day in the principal's office," Connor said nonchalantly.

"Again?" Sarah asked with the disapproving tone of a mother.

"Yes," Connor said in a deadpan voice.

"What did you do?" Sara asked.

"Nothing," Connor replied. His tone implied: 'that's all I have to say about that.'

I figured it was this type of comment that likely got him in trouble in the first place. A mom would have put on her attorney hat and started the inquisition, but Sarah did not. She kept the questions non-confrontational.

"How long were you in there?" Sara inquired.

"Most of the day," Connor said, unaffected.

The boy's younger sister chimed in. "The principal's office is so scary!"

"What did you do while you were in the office?" Sarah asked.

"Just sat there," Conner replied.

That was it. End of discussion. Sarah looked at me and rolled her eyes. I was giggling to myself at Connor's brashness at the ripe old age of five.

Unsolicited, Haley asked me, "Did you know I had two ancestors that were bitten by snakes?"

"No," I told her.

Confidently, she replied, "I had one ancestor that opened up a suitcase and a snake jumped out and bit him on his hand!"

"No kidding," I said.

Her eyes got big and she said, "No I am not kidding! They were like my great, great, grandparents."

I smiled and Haley went on. "My second ancestor was standing in the forest, when a snake dropped from a tree and bit his neck."

"Did they survive?" I asked.

The girl looked at me like I was stupid and said, "Of course not, they are dead!"

I looked at Sarah and smiled. She opened up her hands in a gesture that said, 'See, I told you!'

As a dad with kids of my own, I wish I had written down some of the crazy things they've said over the years. Whenever I'm around younger ones, like those two characters from Pinewood, I don't want to miss the opportunity to engage with them, and document their cleverness if I can. I'm always amazed at how advanced and brilliant kids truly are.

Children not only say the darndest things, they are our reality check. They will entertain, frustrate, and surprise you in ways you could never have imagined. If you're having a crummy day, I suggest sitting down and having a conversation with them. I promise your mood will get better.

MUSKRAT LOVE

"It's okay to tell them no sometimes, too, you know. Moms need to be tough."
-Margo, Despicable Me 3

The muskrat is a medium-sized semiaquatic rodent native to North America that was later introduced in parts of Europe, Asia, and South America. This is a fine rodent I suppose, but not a subject that love songs should be written about.

"I'm doing it," the woman in my rearview mirror said with an evil twinkle in her eye.

"You better not!" the girl shouted with embarrassment.

"Oh, I'm going to do it for sure, and there's nothing you can do to stop me," the woman happily replied.

"I hate you, I really do," the girl grumbled in disgust.

That's how the conversation started between a mom and her daughter entering my car. The girl, a freshman in high school, was three shades of red in the face, and kept glancing nervously at me to see if I was listening to their conversation.

As Mom got in, she flashed me a wry smile, the kind only parents would understand. It somehow contained multiple messages at once: Watch this. Kids are a pain in the ass. What can you do?

"What's your name, driver?" Mom inquired.

"Brian," I replied.

"Brian, what do you think of this song?" she asked.

Her daughter immediately interrupted. "Mom, I'm begging you. Stop!"

Again, the self-conscious girl looked desperately in the rearview mirror to see what I was going to say.

Mom started pushing buttons on her cell phone as her daughter tried desperately to grab it, trying to stop what was inevitably going to happen. Mom was one step ahead of her, and shifted the phone from her left hand to her right, out of the reach of the flailing girl.

"This is my daughter's favorite song," Mom told me with a straight face.

"I swear, Mom. If you do, I'm never going to speak to you again!" the young lady exclaimed.

Mom cued up the song anyway, and the familiar, but not-so-pleasant sound of the Captain and Tennille started playing. Daggers shot from the daughter's eyes. She crossed her arms and immediately assumed a pouty look as I heard the familiar lines:

Love. Love will keep us together. Think of me babe, whenever. Some sweet-talking girl comes along, singing her song…

"Hey Brian," Mom said, getting my attention.

I looked in the car mirror and Mom gave me a collaborative wink.

And then she began to sing...*loudly*. It didn't take me more than a second to understand her gesture. I joined in. Mom and I were serenading the uncomfortable daughter, who at this point, was beside herself with humiliation.

Together we sang it out. *"You. You belong to me now. Ain't gonna set you free now. When those girls start hanging around, talking me down, hear with your heart and you won't hear a sound, just stop (stop)..."*

This is where Mom got creative. She started using hand gestures for each "stop" in the song, extending her arm forward and raising her hand. Of course, I joined her and did the same, one hand on the wheel, one gesturing with the song.

"'Cause I really love, you stop, I'll be thinking of you, Look in my heart and let love keep us together."

We finished our duet, Mom and I laughing hysterically.

If the poor girl could have magically disappeared, I'm sure she would have. Instead, she slunk so far into the seat I couldn't see her anymore. Mom was not insensitive, she just had a warped sense of humor that I appreciated, especially having a teenage girl myself. She asked me if I had children and I told her about my daughter and son. My daughter was a sophomore at the time, and the girl, upon hearing this, sat up in her seat to listen.

After our song rendition, Mom and I started up a conversation.

"My daughter and I share a passion for music. We share songs, I introduce her to classic rock, country and blues, and she turns me on to indie music," I told them.

"That's super cool," Mom told me. "My daughter likes indie music too. But her favorite is Motown."

"Wow, that's impressive," I said honestly. "My daughter also likes

Motown. We listen to a lot of Marvin Gaye and Stevie Wonder," I added.

Upon hearing this, the girl joined in the discussion. She was sweet, intelligent and very knowledgeable about music.

"Marvin Gaye is the best," the teenager stated emphatically. "But you know who I really like?"

"Who?" I asked, thrilled that we were all talking about music together.

"The Temptations!" she declared.

"I love the Temptations," I agreed. *"Papa Was a Rollin' Stone* is one of my favorite songs," I told her. This was absolutely true.

"I like that song too, it has a great intro," the girl concurred. "You know what one of my favorite Temptations' songs is?"

"What?" I inquired.

"My Girl," she answered proudly.

"That's a great song, a classic," I told her.

Mom jumped in at that comment, and asked her daughter, "Why don't you sing it for us?"

"No, I can't," the girl said sheepishly.

Mom ignored her daughter's comment and instantly put on the Temptations song and like clockwork the two started singing along. This was pretty cool. I was receiving a private concert by a couple of strangers in my car.

The two sang, "I've got sunshine on a cloudy day. When it's cold outside I've got the month of May…."

Then Mom stopped singing. Her daughter looked at her and she nodded, at which point the girl sang the rest of the song by herself, unashamed, hitting every word and tone perfectly. She had a remarkably smooth and silky voice. Music was obviously a strong bond the two shared together. It was endearing.

After the song ended, Mom shifted the conversation back to the uncomfortable subject they'd entered the car with. She must have satiated her sweet emotion and the devious side was back.

"What were the worst songs ever recorded?" she asked no one in particular.

I had to think about the question. Thinking back, Miley Cyrus instantly came to mind.

"Wrecking Ball," I stated. "Every time I see that stupid video, I think of the memes with the goat bleating," I said laughing.

They both laughed.

"That goat meme still cracks me up," the girl added with a smile.

"Afternoon Delight!" Mom shouted.

We all agreed.

"Mickey, by Toni Basil!" the girl shouted.

We all started singing that horrid tune and laughed.

"Speaking of Miley Cyrus, how about *Achy, Breaky Heart* by Miley's dad?" I said.

The mom agreed, "Yep, that's a good one, I mean bad one."

"Morning Train by Sheena Easton," the mom stated proudly.

"That's a terrible song," I replied.

"How about *Lady in Red*," I offered. "I don't know who it's by, but it sucks!"

"Macarena," the girl added. "What makes you guys start dancing to that lame song?"

The mother and I looked at each other at broke out in laughter.

"I have another one," the girl stated. "Milli Vanilli's *Girl You Know It's True.*"

"Awful," Mom replied. "They were so fake and got caught lip synching, remember? This is it. *Loving You* by Minnie Riperton," she added, matter-of-factly.

Both the daughter and I started nodding our heads in unison.

Mom quickly searched YouTube and played the song. "I'm playing it," she said.

"No, don't Mom. It's so bad," her daughter pleaded.

Once the song started, we couldn't help ourselves. We sang along, and even mimicked the high-pitch climax to the best of our abilities. The three of us laughed so hard we were crying.

Then the daughter dropped the big bomb. The worst of the worst, all-time, most irritating song in the history of music.

"I've got it," the young woman said surely.

Her mother and I looked at each other and in unison said, "Worse than *Loving You?*"

"Yes," the girl stated. *"Muskrat Love!"*

"Oh my goodness," Mom said. "That is it!" Of course, she found the song and played it.

"Muskrat, Muskrat, candle light. Doing the town and doing it right in the evening. It's pretty pleasing. Muskrat Suzie, Muskrat Sam, Do the jitterbug out in Muskrat Land and they shimmy... Sam is so skinny."

Together, we sang a few verses and hummed the parts we didn't know. Singing with these two was musical bliss, despite the fact that we were singing one of the worst tunes in musical history.

As a driver, I didn't relate with passengers like this very often, but when I did, it was a wonderful and rare moment of connection, camaraderie, and unabashed joy. One that was not soon forgotten.

In parting, Mom laughed and told me she was going to play *My Heart Will Go On,* by Celine Dion.

I replied, "If you do, I'm going to charge you double!"

YOUR DOG ATE WHAT?

I will not let the dogs out.
I will not let the dogs out.
I will not let the dogs out.
[Written on the chalkboard by Bart, as part of his punishment]

-Bart Simpson, The Simpsons

A Lyft request arrived early one Friday evening in the Japantown district of Downtown San Jose. Downtown is my home base, so navigating there was a painless exercise. As I was heading to the location, my phone rang, and the soon-to-be passenger asked, "Do you mind if I bring my dog in the car?"

I happen to love dogs, and assuming it was not the size of a Great Dane, had no trouble obliging. Nothing against big dogs, but a Prius and a colossal canine were simply not a good fit.

"Of course," I happily replied and followed my GPS to the destination.

I pulled up to a large apartment complex and parked. Most rideshare travelers take a minute or two longer on weekends, as there are typically more passengers per trip or last-minute cocktails to be consumed before heading out. Over the years, my patience has become Zen-like. Need more time? No problem, just let me know. I'll watch *Curb Your Enthusiasm* on YouTube while I wait.

Weekend nights can generate almost any kind of rider, so I had no expectations. As I was checking my emails, a boisterous noise startled me, a sound only a large crowd can generate. Thirty people filtered out of the building, and a young couple finally emerged from the entourage. They walked slowly to my car, a small Chihuahua in the man's arms.

As the two got in, the unmistakable smell of marijuana permeated the car. This scenario is not unusual these days, as pot is legal in California, and there are numerous dispensaries on what seems like every block in San Jose.

Tiffany and Brad were typical millennials, both in their late twenties. She was a cute petite blonde, with ripped jeans, halter top, and bubbly personality. Brad was more reserved in his jeans, white V-neck shirt, and trendy brown lace-up boots. He sported a signature unkempt beard, the preferred fashion statement for men his age.

Brad was holding the dog carefully, petting it gingerly, and speaking to it in the most gentle of voices.

"It's okay, Riley. It's okay," he repeated over and over.

This was strange. Most people don't speak so delicately to their animals, so I knew something was off. I turned to look at my little passenger, and observed the most unenthusiastic animal I have ever seen. No tail wagging, no expression.

Once settled, I addressed them with my standard greeting, reserved for all but the very young and very old.

"Hi guys, how's it going?" I inquired with trepidation.

Tiffany was very friendly and spoke up immediately.

"We're...awesome...but...Riley...is...not...so...well."

The deliberateness of her words made me stop for a moment. To say this girl's speech was unhurried would be generous. If you spell out M-O-L-A-S-S-E-S as slowly as you can, you'll get the gist.

Shaking my head in confusion, I continued, "Oh, I'm sorry to hear that. What's wrong with the little guy?"

Tiffany paused, as if she didn't understand the question or perhaps forgot the topic. Moments later I would realize it was the latter. After a minute of deep concentrated effort, in a tone louder than needed, she blurted out, "OKAY, I CONFESS!"

I immediately started laughing. "What are you confessing?" I asked.

"We're both stoned and can't drive," she said in a lazy drawl. "That's why we called you!"

In reality, the pair was more than a little high. They were both in a total haze. I recall my early high school days, operating in a similar green fog. This severely intoxicated state comes from smoking large quantities of pot in a very short period of time— and then smoking some more.

As I casually looked into my rearview mirror, I met two sets of bloodshot eyes, a scarlet hue Bob Marley would have been proud of. This explained the girl's sluggish tempo.

"No worries," I said snickering. "You did the right thing by calling Lyft. I drive people every night in some state of intoxication. That's why I'm here."

Undeterred, Tiffany continued. "No, you don't understand. See that big crowd right there?"

"Sure," I said.

"We were hosting a party for all our friends. There was a big bag of party materials, enough for the group. Everybody was having a great time," she stated proudly.

"Go on," I urged.

"Suddenly, we heard yelling from the back room, and people started calling us. We immediately ran to the rear of the house, and discovered Riley walking in circles. Then he just fell over, and one of our friends began apologizing to us," she exclaimed.

I was looking at Tiffany, my mouth wide open in shock.

"He just laid there and wouldn't move!" Tiffany was shouting now, clearly upset.

Brad finished the story in a disgusted tone: "The damn dog ate our stash!"

My eyes darted from the couple, to the dog, then back at the couple. Looking at the little guy, he looked remarkably like them: heavy eyelids, bloodshot eyes, and listless. Riley's tongue was hanging out of his expressionless mouth and all four of his legs were splayed out on his owner's lap. Imagine a canine version of Cheech Marin in *Up in Smoke*.

The uncertainty of what was happening quickly became crystal clear.

"He ate the entire bag?" I asked.

"About half of it," Tiffany replied.

"Friggin' dog ate our stash," Brad mumbled again in that same disgruntled tone.

"Oh my God, are you saying both the dog and its owners are

totally wasted?" I asked, stating the obvious.

The couple answered simultaneously, "Yes!"

The car erupted with laughter.

There we were, driving down the roads in San Jose, all three of us hysterical to the point of tears. We must have made quite a scene for the passing cars.

It's a good thing a California Highway Patrol car didn't pull up next to us at a stoplight, or he would have surely pulled us over. One look at my passengers, combined with the unmistakable aroma of ganja, and we would all have had some explaining to do at the police station.

My mind sometimes works in twisted ways. All I could think of at the moment was the cartoon character Scooby-Doo saying, 'Rut Roh, Scooby ate the wrong snack!' I started to laugh again, which in retrospect, was totally inappropriate considering the circumstances. However, I really couldn't help myself. I was desperately trying to hold it together, failing miserably in controlling my now constant giggling. And I wasn't even the one under the influence.

Acknowledging my faux pas, I quickly apologized. "I'm really sorry, guys. I am not laughing at you, just the situation. This is one of the most unusual rides I have ever been on."

My comment helped relax Riley's owners, and Tiffany addressed my concern. "It's all good. We just want to make sure Riley is okay."

Nervous silence interrupted the good mood, as we all realized that Riley was likely seeing colors at this stage.

"So where are we headed?" I asked, as the ride only listed the address of the destination, not the name.

"The vet," they both answered.

Off we drove to the doggy doctor. I'm sure the vet had to restrain himself from laughing when this trio walked into the examining room. I can only imagine the challenge these two owners faced when filling out registration paperwork.

In the end, I was confident that Riley would be fine after getting the cannabis pumped out of his pint-sized stomach. It's a shame they couldn't have done the same for Riley's owners.

What do dogs dream of, I wonder, when they are high as a kite? A Fred Flintstone-sized bone or an all-you-can-eat bacon bar? We'll never know the answer to this timeless question, or Riley's fate for that matter. However, assuming he made it through, he had a helluva tale to tell his dog buddies.

DREAMERS

Optimism is attractive. Creative optimism is infectious. Because Silicon Valley offers so much opportunity, and the infrastructure to support creative ideas, I inevitably ran across people with fresh new ideas who were involved in some sort of grand venture, or who were employed in professions I didn't know even existed.

This made for some interesting discussions. Having a layman's understanding of the startup world helped instigate some of these conversations. Many entrepreneurs I transported were surprised by the detailed questions I asked about their businesses. I even met with several of my passengers for coffee, and pitched ideas of my own. Most were accommodating; all were extremely intelligent.

Yet the success of many of these riders was not entirely due to ambition. Being in the right place at the right time was also a key ingredient for those who experienced wealth beyond most people's wildest fantasies. I was lucky to have driven a few of these individuals and had the chance to speak to them about their experiences. Some came from other countries to the land of technology, in search of the Holy Grail—or at least, the interest of a venture capital firm.

What I discovered is that no two dreamers were alike.

TIMING IS EVERYTHING IN SILICON VALLEY

"Most of life's burdens, with a little help, can become a gift."
-Master Gregory, Seventh Son

I would be remiss if I didn't include a story about the dynamic area I call home, the San Francisco Bay Area, a region full of such infectious creativity it feels palpable. Entrepreneurial innovation is abundant all over NorCal, especially in areas like Palo Alto, Mountain View and San Francisco.

One can overhear discussions about new ventures everywhere. Whether you're sipping Blue Bottle Coffee (one of my favorites) at the HanaHaus in Palo Alto, eating breakfast at Buck's in Woodside, enjoying a glass of Pinot Noir at Madera restaurant at the Rosewood Sand Hill in Menlo Park, or eating sushi at Nobu in the revitalized Epiphany Hotel, the area boasts an endless supply of fresh ideas and aspiring billionaires.

As an Uber or Lyft driver in this part of the world, I picked up people from network meetups, technology conventions, and corporate power dinners. I dropped passengers off at startup incubators such as Plug and tech mammoths like Facebook. Not much thought went into these trips, although I never know when I might be giving a ride to the next Mark Zuckerberg or Steve Jobs.

These ambitious riders always had an agenda, and generated some interesting conversations. Most entrepreneurs fell into two categories: engineers and managers. Engineers were often more introverted, and spoke their own coding lingo. A conversation with two engineers was like listening to a foreign language, and they were always trying to find a "bug" in the latest software. Technology managers, on the other hand, had a completely different vernacular, using terms like KPI, API, SaaS, CAPM, SWOT Analysis and DEVOPS. If you don't know what those acronyms mean, don't worry—I didn't either. Google them, and you'll be as confused as when you started.

Despite the bounty of accomplished people living and working in the Bay Area, very few are able to reach the technology pinnacle. Talent by itself can get one in the door, but success is by no means guaranteed. Here in Silicon Valley, *timing is everything*. If you add talent and a bit of luck, rock stardom is yours for the taking.

In Northern California, at any given moment, there are a million variables in action. Venture firms are analyzing hundreds of deals, expanding technology companies are looking for software solutions, and your collegiate buddy just became the CEO of a new startup. Timing determines whether two companies execute a successful merger, whether an angel investor invests in a disrupting product, and whether a seasoned executive secures that coveted senior position. Timing can mean the difference between Uber wealth (pun intended) and simply working to maintain a comfortable living.

Timing also has the power to shape company policy and dictate the path it eventually travels. If a new business is able to secure capital, especially in its infancy, it can then hire and scale quickly. If the same company then decides to further expand by offering shares to the public, the price per share (and the value of the initial offering) is partly influenced by what? Say it with me, *timing is everything*.

This dynamic applies not only to deal making, but it also trickles down to the talented staff. If an employee is in *exactly* the right place when needed, dreams become reality.

One passenger, Timo, was, in the truest sense, a Xennial. Hip in a beatnik kind of way, he played the part well: dark beard, disheveled hair, unassuming and confident, but not a hint of arrogance. At first appearance, you might think he was an artist, or a musician in an indie band. When he walked up to my car from a popular restaurant in Mountain View he looked spent. Surprisingly, he also had a smile on his face. I couldn't tell whether his expression was from a 100-hour week or too many beers.

"Hi Timo! How are you tonight?" I asked as he stepped into the car.

"I'm exhausted. I've been up for a few days," he said in a voice reserved for weekend partiers, interns at Google, and startup founders.

The variety of people who got into my car was the best part of being a driver. Each traveler was unique and often had a fascinating story to tell. Chatting with my customers made the trips seem shorter and definitely more enjoyable.

Many people loved to talk about their challenges, their vacations, their triumphs, even their relationships. My theory is that rideshare drivers are benign and anonymous, like a bartender. As the intake of alcohol increased, the likelihood my car becoming a confessional was greater. Because of this perception, some passengers opened up. There was no judgement, and the possibility of seeing me again was minimal.

When a passenger wanted to chat, I was more than happy to oblige. Small talk comes easily to me, so I decided to stir the conversational pot with Timo, to see if he would share his tale.

"No offense, but you look bone-tired. Binge weekend?" I asked, expecting to hear an account of his debaucheries.

"No, it's not like that. I have been in New York, and my company just went public. In fact, I was at the podium when they banged the gavel and announced our addition to the exchange." I would later learn his firm was just listed on the New York Stock Exchange and issued $175 Million worth of stock in its initial public offering.

"That is exciting!" I said sincerely. "Are you an entrepreneur?"

"Not in the truest sense of the word. I am an engineer," he said flatly.

"How does an engineer end up on the IPO stage?" I asked, anxious to hear more about his journey.

As Timo began to tell me his story, I quickly realized how humble and approachable he was, both admirable traits in my mind. Married, with a ten-year-old son, he was enthusiastic while describing his family. Clearly, they were the center of his world. When he started his career he was also juggling startup responsibilities, which is no simple task because of the long hours and high stress of a new venture.

For those not familiar with this unique world, startups offer new employees low-priced shares (ownership) in the company, in exchange for a reduced salary. However, these shares cannot be sold immediately. Instead, they are restricted, and released incrementally, usually over a four-year time period. This compensation strategy motivates new staff to continue to work hard, in the hopes that a different company will eventually buy their shares at a much higher price when their firm is sold. The other possibility is the original company goes public instead of being sold, and the shares can then be sold on the open market.

If either of these events take place, those who hold this early-stage compensation ("equity") stand to make a fortune. As an example, Travis Kalanick was the co-founder and former CEO of Uber and held 22.6 million shares of company stock. The transportation firm went public, and in a two-month period, he sold a majority of his very low-priced shares for $2.5 Billion. However, a score this big is rare. Many new startups don't hit their fifth year of operation.

In Silicon Valley, to own shares in a deceased startup is almost a rite of passage. There are countless employees in this area who have worked for a technology company that is no longer in business. Many of these firms touted themselves as the next Twitter, LinkedIn, or Snapchat. Fate had a different idea.

My tired passenger continued. "It was 2005, and I was fresh out of grad school. My wife and I had just moved to Palo Alto for her job, and I was looking for my first job in the technology industry. While attending a recruiting event, a cloud-storage company approached me. Cloud computing was a relatively new concept, and people were still skeptical of the service. I also spoke to a conventional storage company that was well established, and discussed opportunities with them as well."

"So the cloud company made you an offer?" I asked, intrigued by his account.

"Actually, I was lucky. Both companies made me an offer," he said deferentially.

You could see Timo reminiscing, like he hadn't thought about how he had arrived at this point. This *Hero's Journey*, the strange path that led him to where he was now, rested on a single decision— a fortunate moment in time.

"The traditional storage company paid a higher salary, had a predictable work schedule, and offered minimal equity. The cloud storage company had more responsibility, a lower salary, and offered a large amount of ownership. The 80+ hour work week with the startup seemed daunting. However, the autonomy and advancement possibilities were appealing. I was so confused!" he admitted.

Mesmerized at this point, I sympathized, having also been involved with a startup that received an early round of funding, burned through the money, and died a premature death. "Please continue," I eagerly asked.

"I lamented for days over which company to choose. After analyzing it ten different ways, and many conversations with my wife, I was still undecided. I honestly considered flipping a coin, that's how close the two positions were in my mind," Timo emphasized.

He kept talking and I wasn't going to stop him. "I had already prepared myself mentally for long hours. So I chose the cloud-based company and took a leap of faith. Fortunate for me!"

He laughed sheepishly, like he couldn't believe it.

"You must be an excellent engineer?" I asked honestly, assuming that if a technology company hired him as one of their earliest employees, he was brilliant.

"I just think my timing was good," he said. "Don't get me wrong. I can code with the best of them, but the company is full of very talented people."

At this juncture, we were thirty minutes into the ride, and passing San Francisco International Airport on the way to his home in 'The City.' Enthralled with his story, I wanted more details.

Suddenly, there was a break in the conversation. Complete silence. The pause was so abrupt, it was almost uncomfortable. I immediately looked in my rearview mirror to see if Timo was asleep. My vision limited at night, I strained to see what my passenger was doing. To my surprise, he was just sitting there, staring ahead, in a total state of contemplation.

"Are you okay?" I asked, concerned.

"Oh my God, my life just changed," he said.

Timo had an epiphany right in my back seat. He just realized his life *would* look very different now. Timo was now a multi-millionaire—likely ten times over would be my guess. Financial freedom and multi-generational wealth were a given. Retirement, buying a new house or car, giving to charity—all were possible. The reality was, he could do whatever he wanted. I can only imagine what he was thinking.

Imagine that a friend persuades you to buy a lottery ticket, and you are reluctant. You concede, only to discover the next day you won the grand prize. This must have been similar to the overwhelming emotions Timo was feeling. He could have taken the safe route and went to work for the established storage company. Instead, he took a risk with a firm that had less of a track history, in return for a larger percentage of ownership. In the end, this was his winning ticket—and his timing was perfect.

This engineer was the twelfth employee and held the title of Global Manager. He now ran several large teams of talented engineers. His company has millions of users, including many of the Fortune 500. The best thing was he could cash in his newfound wealth whenever he wanted, by easily selling his shares.

The gravity in the car was palpable. I could almost feel his disbelief. Choked up, his voice was shaky for the next few minutes. So large was this moment, Timo was having a hard time absorbing the gravity of it all. He was trying to comprehend this new information, on the ride home with me.

For just a moment I was caught up in Timo's euphoria—part of his world. My excitement for him was genuine, as here was a regular person who did well, and would have a magnified life because of his hard work and timing. We were both grinning ear-to-ear.

This story is not unique. The area I drove was full of mavericks who have traveled this entrepreneurial road before, carefully avoiding the pitfalls along the way. It was common to see young men and women who looked barely old enough to hold a license, drive by in a Porsche, Ferrari, or Model S 90D Tesla. Timo was not the first risk taker I had in my car, but he was first person whose life changed in such close proximity to mine.

Was Timo an entrepreneur? From my point of view, I would say yes. In the early 2000s, you had to have an adventurous spirit if you took a job with a young technology firm. Startups weren't as common as they are today. These new companies often didn't have a track history and the firms that invested in these new ideas were not as abundant. It was a new frontier, uncharted territory.

There's no question, success in the volatile technology industry means you must embrace risk and have a bit of luck. Yet this is not always enough. Success is not always based on being a brilliant engineer or an experienced founder. As Timo said, there are a lot of talented people here. The Bay Area, and other tech-rich areas, such as Austin and Seattle, are fickle environments. Companies that were high flyers yesterday, like Blackberry, Napster, MySpace and Netscape, are no longer in business.

Many of us have heard the saying, 'I'd rather be lucky than good.' In my opinion, to really make it in this fantasy land we call Silicon Valley, it helps to have a bit more than luck. To get to critical mass, you need to hit the Trifecta. You must have talent, optimal luck, and need that longshot to come in—the horse named timing. If the planets align and you have all three together, you likely have a winner. The unfathomable payout.

LOOKING OVER THE EDGE

"Like Papa Wallenda said, life is on the wire. The rest is just waiting."
-Mike McDermott, Rounders

Imagine you are standing on a cliff, looking over the edge into infinity, wind in your face, and feet on the edge. In order to realize your wildest dreams, you have to jump. Take a leap of faith. Could you do it?

Few of us have a job that we love. Instead, we settle into a profession that generates needed income for our families, gives us a comfortable lifestyle, and provides stability. These are honorable reasons, but many people are left unhappy or unfulfilled, wishing they were doing something different.

Aspirations or reality. Risk or practicality. Guarantees or uncertainty. Pivot or stay where you are. All are difficult choices. If you could reinvent yourself, do exactly what you always dreamed about, what would that look like?

I met someone who was given a chance to do just that—mold his future exactly as he envisioned. He was also facing one the biggest decisions of his life.

The young man had just arrived at the Oakland Airport when I received the request. After a long night working in San Francisco,

I was spent, having come from my house in San Jose earlier that day. City driving is demanding, and involves more focus, energy and stamina.

In this blurry-eyed state, I was not keen about another ride. Fares at this hour usually involved an exhausted traveler and little discussion, my ability to stay between the lines was questionable. A quiet car, late at night, is peaceful. Unless, of course, you can't see straight.

Conversely, money talks. If a driver can pick up a passenger going in the same direction, and it is close to quitting time, it is foolish not to take advantage of this opportunity. After all, you're not driving for fun.

I took the ride.

When I pulled curbside, the young man was ready for me. After loading his bags, we left the airport and headed towards the 880 Freeway. I was pleasantly surprised that he was talkative and lived about ten minutes from me; we were about a 40-minute drive to his door.

"Where are you coming from?" I asked, partly to start a conversation, but also to keep from falling asleep.

"Detroit," he said.

"That's not a city I hear often. Do you have family there?" I inquired.

"No, I was in a tournament."

"Really? What kind of tournament?" I asked, my curiosity piqued. I had played in many poker tournaments in the Bay Area, Las Vegas and Los Angeles.

"I was playing in an international gaming competition," he said matter-of-factly.

"How did you do?" I asked with interest.

"I placed sixth," he said, in a tone that hinted at both pride and disappointment.

Damian was lean, gregarious, and affable—twenty-five, at best. You don't often meet someone with such an unusual hobby, so I continued to probe him about his trip. I was met with a burst of genuine enthusiasm, the kind that comes from being passionate about something. Both educated and charismatic, he loved what he did, and it showed.

What I learned is that Damian was a world-class video gamer. (To assure anonymity, I am not disclosing the specific game.) Ranked in the top 15 globally, he had competed in almost 150 tournaments, many held in other countries.

He also had a secure, well-paying job as a gaming engineer. Being under thirty and successful, he could have assumed an arrogant, over-confident attitude. Instead, he was self-effacing, analytical and laid back. Refreshing for such a young man.

My personal experience with the video gaming industry was almost non-existent, unless you count constantly barking at my 15-year-old son to disconnect from whatever game he was playing and join the conversation. However, I did know that gaming is part of our culture. You would have a difficult time finding households that don't have an Xbox or PlayStation.

I would later learn that gaming is not just an online community, it's a digital tribe, with 2.5 billion across the globe. Hence the birth of eSports: competitive gaming tournaments held in huge stadiums, where the best players compete for prestige and significant cash prizes. Broadcast globally, with associated streaming fees, one such tournament, the International Dota 2 Championships, the Superbowl of gaming, offered a first place prize of a staggering $15.5 Million in 2019.

Some professional gaming influencers, called streamers, made more money per year than celebrities. One player, Shroud, had 6.18 million subscribers on YouTube, and made more than $100,000 per month on subscription fees alone.

If that wasn't enough, affiliate marketing, corporate sponsorships, and merchandising added to streamers' annual compensation. To the younger generation, these players were modern-day rock stars.

All of this was making life for my young rider, Damian, more complicated. His hobby had presented some interesting decisions, not all painless. Because of his tournament success, his sponsor had asked him to move to the team house in Los Angeles—an all-inclusive house where gaming strategies could be discussed, techniques shared, and competitors analyzed. An ideal environment for an aspiring pro to develop his skills.

We discussed what it would be like if he moved to LA.

"Man, how fun would that be? I could be so focused and could get even better!" Damian exclaimed, his demeanor becoming animated.

"How much traveling would that involve?" I asked.

"I would be traveling all over the world and could develop a name for myself in the international gaming community," he replied excitedly.

His excitement was intoxicating, his enthusiasm infectious.

"There are huge competitions in Asia: Seoul and Tokyo are big. Tacna, Peru has a large tournament. Gothenburg, Paris, Los Angeles, Orlando, Boston, and Denver. We even compete in San Jose."

"How does extensive traveling like that sound to you?" I asked, anticipating the answer.

Damian hesitated a bit before answering. "I would miss my parents and my girlfriend. It would be really hard to leave them. But, oh my God, it would be so cool! What's not to like? I can't think of anything I would rather do more."

Deciding whether to leave the security of home in pursuit of greater success is an ageless quandary. Damian's job presented one of the biggest challenges with jumping into the unknown. Having worked hard to get to where he was, he was drawing a six-figure paycheck.

"If I was just starting my career, the choice would be much easier. But I make good money. I really like what I do. I get paid to play games and make them better. How do I walk away from that security"" he asked rhetorically.

This young engineer lived at home and was prudently saving money. He helped his family financially and had a close relationship with his mother. Good kid, strong morals. He kept talking and I didn't want to stop him.

"My mom is a big influence in my life. We didn't have a lot of money growing up," he admitted honestly. "She worked hard to make sure I attended college."

Understandably, he felt a moral obligation to his mother, whose hard work allowed him to develop a successful career.

"When I started playing video games, she tolerated it. I told her I was going to compete, and she wasn't that excited about it. I still don't think she is totally on board," he laughed. "She has always been supportive, but on the condition that it remain a hobby."

"She is understandably protective. That's what moms do," I said.

"I know, I get it," he acknowledged. "The other day, I hinted at competing more and she told me, 'No way. You have worked hard. Leaving a consistent paycheck is crazy.'"

From a parental standpoint, this viewpoint made perfect sense. Damian had a good job, health insurance and financial stability. Everything a young person needed. To further complicate matters, he also had a long-time girlfriend—not an ideal fit for a gamer on the road. When we got to this subject, I could tell it was weighing heavy on his mind.

"We've gone out for some time now, and I don't want to hurt her," he said sadly.

I didn't want to push him on this issue, so I left it alone. Damian got quiet for a moment as he pondered his relationship. Big decisions for a young man, and a short time to make up his mind.

I was emotionally involved by this point, trying desperately to stay neutral. Truth be told, I was having a hard time. This young man had a shot at living his dream at the highest level. Most of us only get to watch our heroes from a distance. He had the opportunity to be one.

In a former life, competitive poker was my occupation. Although I never achieved elite level, I did make a respectable living doing something I loved. It was one of the best periods in my life. I wanted to give Damian some personal perspective.

"A few years back, I had a friend win a big poker tournament in Las Vegas, and we shared the prize money," I told him. "The casino pays winners with chips, and you have to exchange those chips for cash."

Damian was listening intently.

"I was waiting to get paid, and my friend threw me a small stack of chips, which I instinctively caught. 'What's this?' I asked my friend. 'How's it feel to hold a half million dollars in your hand?'

my friend asked me with a smile. 'This is a half-million dollars?' I asked. 'Yes!' my friend said."

"It was surreal," I told Damian. I could feel my neutrality leaning way to one side. Damian laughed, but you could tell the wheels were turning. We discussed alternate ways to make money if he chose to travel with the team.

"There are other ways you could generate more income. You could stream online and do affiliate marketing," I suggested.

Damian was way ahead of me. He already had 36,000 Twitter followers and an admirable social media presence. I was preaching to the choir.

"Yes, I have some ideas," he replied. "Gamers don't always live the healthiest lifestyle. They sit for long periods of time and eat crappy food. I was thinking of developing a series of health-related videos specifically for players."

I quickly realized he was two steps in front of me.

"What's more important to you, a consistent paycheck or taking a chance at making a living doing what you love?" I asked, trying desperately to sound unbiased.

"Not sure. I know what I want to do, but I have so much here," he said with a heavy sigh.

"Can I ask you another hard question?" I asked honestly.

"Sure," he replied.

"I'm not saying one decision is better than the next," I prefaced.

"Go ahead and ask me," he said.

"Could you live with yourself if you didn't take a shot at it? I mean, could you take the practical route, continue your career, build a retirement, and watch gaming from a distance? With no regrets? If you can say yes, the decision is much easier," I said.

"You know something, as much as I like my job, it's the same thing every day. There is no adrenaline. Competing is a rush"

"I've been there, it's pretty cool," I said truthfully.

"I just don't know, but my deadline is coming up," he stated. "They want me to decide soon, and move into the house by next summer. It's a big risk."

A big risk indeed.

"Sometimes you have to go with your heart. Decisions this size are never easy," I said as an afterthought, trying to console him.

Although we talked incessantly for most of the trip, the last ten minutes were quiet. I knew Damian was at a juncture in his life, and faced choices that would have huge implications in his future. He was looking over the edge, wrestling with opposing forces. Trying to please those he cared most about, and listening to the screaming voice telling him to jump. Damien wanted reassurance that the next step was the right one. Unfortunately, life doesn't work that way, especially in those rare times when it's magnified.

I wished Damian the best in his quest for the truth. Secretly, I hoped that whatever road he chose, it would be the right one for him.

Update: This story was originally written in 2017. I recently checked on Damian's tournament progress. He jumped off that proverbial cliff, and is still competing at the highest level in the eSports industry.

PERSISTENCE

"Why do we fall sir? So that we can learn to pick ourselves up."
-Alfred, Batman Begins

To get a desired result, sometimes brilliance is necessary—perfect execution. Other times, a little persistence is all it takes. This adage also applies to operating a vehicle, whether you are a professional Lyft driver or simply getting your own car down the road. The most important thing is not how you got there, only that you arrived.

Passengers have commented that their ride with me seemed smooth and effortless. I enjoy driving, and late night was my favorite time to work. One might describe my style as assertive but safe, and not overly-cautious. Having completed over 20,000 plus rides, I knew the Bay Area well and had developed the ability to avoid potential road hazards.

If my rider wasn't chatty, I often got into a driving zone. A calm takes over, an autopilot that happens only after the sun goes down and traffic subsides. In fact, there were occasional rides when I don't remember getting from point A to B. The trip starts, and fifteen minutes later it is over, with little recollection of passing streets and traffic lights.

On a quiet Tuesday night, I had such a night, when the mental cruise-control was obviously turned on.

Anne was a sweet Filipino woman in her mid-fifties who requested a ride one sleepy evening. Most of my business was over and the end of my shift was near. When she first got into the car, we exchanged the usual greetings but not much more.

On first impression, Anne seemed a bit reserved, which isn't that unusual for a mature woman who secures a personal taxi late in the evening. I left her alone and focused on getting her to the destination. The car silent, the humming of the road intoxicating—in my zone.

Unbeknownst to me, Anne must have picked up on my mellow trance-state and was carefully observing my navigation. It startled me when she broke the silence and asked, "How long have you been driving?"

Thinking I was speeding or had just run a stop sign, I hesitated a bit before answering her. After a quick rewind, mentally checking the last few streets for errors, and a complicated multi-decade calculation, I answered her reluctantly.

"I have been doing rideshare a little over four years," I replied. "But if you are asking in general, about 41 years, since age 15."

"I need some advice," Anne stated. "You seem very comfortable in the car. I have driven for only two years, and have taken instructions several times a week. However, I'm not doing very well."

Driving for a living is unquestionably a social outlet and can often be therapeutic for both passenger and driver. I was happy to counsel Anne and answer her questions.

"Really sorry to hear that," I replied honestly. "Why are you having challenges?"

"I have to cut back on my lessons because of my promotion at work. Should I keep taking these classes, if I can only take the course one day a week?" she asked intently.

"I would think any instruction would be helpful," I said, offering support. "Why have you only been driving for two years?"

"Well, before my current position, I was a school principal in the Philippines. But I'm a caregiver now, working graveyard shifts. I only drive a couple of times a week to Los Gatos, where my elder care facility is located," she stated.

Turns out, Anne's commute started from the East Side of San Jose, where I picked her up. Because she traveled at rush hour, her drive entailed moderate-to-serious traffic, with the freeway being the best route most days.

"I only drive side streets" she said matter-of-factly. "No freeway for me. It makes me too nervous!"

"Oh my goodness," I said shocked.

Average driving times in the Bay Area vary, but 30 minutes would be a good estimate from her house to work. Instead, she took side streets and dealt with an indeterminable number of stop lights, not to mention the stress and frustration of dealing with impatient tailgaters, anxious to get to their house at the end of a long workday.

"So how long *does* it take you to get to work?" I asked in disbelief.

"About an hour and a half," she said in a tone that suggested there was nothing unusual about this marathon trek across the valley.

"Wow, that is a long time," I exclaimed.

Anne was comfortable now. "I wouldn't have even tried to get my driver's license, but it's required for my job," she said in a disgusted tone. "Did you know the instructor told me I was the most difficult student at driving school?"

Although she was very amiable and approachable, I would soon find out Anne was more than a little headstrong. Obstinate was the word that came to mind, but I kept this thought to myself. She was on a roll and I wasn't going to slow her down.

"My instructor would always tell me to turn in a certain direction, often through an intersection. I would have to time oncoming traffic! Can you believe that?" she asked defiantly. "I would ask him why can't I turn right and go around the block. It's so much easier."

At the moment, I didn't want to discourage her. But my bigger challenge was trying not to laugh. I wasn't unsympathetic, but it *was* a driving test! I kept listening.

The pace of her speech increased as Anne continued. "He would ask me to please make a U-turn! I told him, 'Oh no, not a U-turn!'" There was no discussion, she would simply refuse to comply with the instructor. Obviously, she felt this refusal to comply was not the least bit unusual.

Then the conversation shifted to the topic of her husband. In retrospect, I'm confident she wanted confirmation that driving was a universal challenge. Smiling widely by this time, I resigned myself that I wasn't going to get another word in until she finished her rant.

"Last week, my husband needed to go to San Francisco. He doesn't drive much, and is a very nervous driver." She said this so confidently, you would have thought she was telling me she had just completed racing lessons from Jeff Gordon. If that wasn't the pot calling the kettle black, I don't know what was.

Of course, I let her continue.

"I decided to go with him. We are driving to the city, maybe twenty minutes from the house, and he makes a wrong turn off a ramp. So there we were, heading *back* to San Jose!"

Looking in the rearview mirror, and despite it being nighttime, I swear I saw Anne roll her eyes. By then, I wasn't hiding my amusement and giggling loudly.

"Do you know what he did then?" she asked incredulously.

I was about to reply, but she didn't wait for me—a conversational snowball. "He drove back home, dropped me off, and left to go see a friend! He then had his *friend* drive him to the city. Can you believe that?" she asked in total disgust.

At that moment, we both started laughing. I was loving this, two strangers, having a funny, friendly conversation on a Lyft ride. It took us a few minutes for us both to stop cackling. Once we did, I was dying to hear what happened with her driving adventure.

I prompted her. "What happened with your driver's license?"

"I didn't get it for more than five years," she answered sheepishly.

"What do you mean? You didn't test again for five years?" I probed.

"Oh, I took the test," she quipped. "Sixteen times!"

"No way, sixteen times?" I couldn't believe what I was hearing.

"Yep, three times every year for five years," she said proudly. "I was so happy when I passed, I kissed the instructor. Every person in the DMV knows my name!"

"Oh my God," I said laughingly, not hiding my amusement.

Anne joined in with a smile. "You are laughing at me."

"Not even close," I said. "I admire your persistence. Most people would have quit after only a few attempts. You took the test sixteen times and prevailed! I am laughing *with* you! That is amazing!"

It took me a few moments to get my head around this. Three times every year for five years plus one. This woman was the most determined person I had ever met. Imagine failing at something for half a decade, and being patient enough to finish. Not to mention, swallowing one's pride takes courage, and having that kind of perseverance takes a very strong will.

Driving was tiresome and frustrating at times, but since I had been driving for so long, it was second nature. Even in traffic, the process was relatively easy. Anne had driven for only two years. I could only imagine how intimidating rush hour was to her.

Anne was a true character, and what a perfect pair she and her husband made. Certain people are just meant for each other. In the end, I told her to keep up with the lessons, that driving would get easier. I sincerely hope this was true in her case.

As drivers, we only get a glimpse into our passengers' lives and rarely have an opportunity to bond with them. Riders like Anne made the memory of unhappy passengers fade quickly, leaving you in a wonderful mood, and reinforcing your belief in the resilient human spirit.

DO YOU FEEL ME?

*"Oh yes, the past can hurt. But you can either run from it, or
learn from it."*
-Rafiki, The Lion King

On a cold and windy evening in 2019, a young rapper I gave
a ride to reminded me that anything was possible. I didn't
realize it then but our conversation would be the catalyst for this
book.

One of the first things I noticed about him was his ethnicity: it
was unusual, an attractive mix of Asian and African-American.
White dreads ran down to his shoulders and framed his golden-
brown face. He wore a red sports jersey, and several thin gold
necklaces tastefully adorned his neck. Black jeans, tennis shoes
and a black wool coat completed his stylish but effortless look.

His facial features were delicate, almost childlike. Sharp
cheekbones highlighted soft, quiet eyes and his distinguishing
feature —a smile, which he only showed a few times. But when
he did, his face lit up. It was beautiful and genuine. I couldn't
help but smile with him. He was tall and lanky, the kind of body a
young man possesses, or one who has not yet seen indulgence. I
would quickly learn it was both.

When he spoke, his voice was almost feminine—quiet and gentle.
A voice that belied his body and didn't match either his attire or

his profession, yet seemed perfectly suited to him. In a word, silky.

Our conversation started generally and quickly accelerated into very personal detail. Arthit was smart; he was deliberate, confident, self-assured, but with a rapper's dialect and a hint of immaturity. Not the kind of immaturity that comes from insecurity but rather, lack of experience.

I quickly learned that Arthit's arduous life journey began before most kids experience their first kiss. He had lived a lifetime by the time we met each other, having experienced the extreme highs of success, and spirit- breaking lows. He was only 24 years old, but he'd skipped past childhood altogether.

I had started the conversation with a simple question: "What do you do, buddy? Are you in school?"

"No, I graduated from high school in an accelerated program when I was 16," he said flatly.

And this brief exchange opened up the floodgates, giving me a glimpse into the life of one of the most inspirational people I have ever met. Arthit's mom was a loving woman, stern but fair, and a bit overprotective, as his father was not around. His household was loving and nurturing, but like many low-income families, his mother had to work several jobs to make ends meet. This meant Arthit had less supervision than he should have. His saving grace was his intelligence, he had a solid head on his shoulders. This single attribute helped him survive without parental guidance, a home, and the worst possible place imaginable. His other saving grace, it turns out, was music.

"I'm a rapper," he added without prompting.

"Really? How long have you been doing music?" I asked, trying to get him to talk more.

"Yeah, I've been rapping since I was 17," he said matter-of-factly. Again, without my solicitation, he added, "Music actually saved my life."

"What do you mean?" I inquired.

As he started talking, I could see that music was this kid's muse. Saying he liked music would be doing him a disservice. He lived it; it was part of his being. And music turned his life around.

"I was pretty headstrong," he admitted. "I love my mom. She's an angel. But we argued a lot. I started running with a tough crowd, you know, hanging around late at night, getting into trouble."

"That happens," I added empathetically.

"At that time, I thought I knew everything. You couldn't tell me anything. So I left and started living on the street."

"Wow, how old were you?" I asked.

"Fifteen," he said casually.

Tragic. Homeless at age 15, he obviously had few options, none of them good ones.

"You know I was in jail?" he asked, again without prompting or shame.

"You were in jail? What for?" I asked, assuming drugs were the reason.

"Yep, for ten months. I was only 17. Armed robbery," he stated.

The statement made me a little nervous as I now had a felon in my car who had committed a crime with a weapon. I paid close attention to his words and demeanor as we continued talking.

"There was no co-defendant," Arthit reported. "So I took the plea, because you know, I had priors. You feel me?" he asked, unexpectedly.

"I do," I said, not knowing the right response.

"Music saved me in jail," he said. "I wrote all day. Every day. I even performed for the other inmates if they asked me."

When his cellmates and other inmates were hustling drugs, he wrote music. Little did Arthit know, this passion for music, even in such a dire environment, would come to define who he was, and give him an identity other than a criminal.

I learned that this young rapper completed his sentence, got out and was put on house arrest. But something had changed: his attitude, his mindset. Determined to never go back to jail, Arthit made up his mind to *not* repeat the same mistakes he had made before going in. Because he was steadfast in his determination to get out of the mess he had created, he did some needed soul-searching. More importantly, he decided that failure was not in his future.

The solution he came up with? Music. Which is when, he told me, the real work began. "I spent 22 hours in my room every day, because I was only allowed to go outside for a few hours, around the house."

Most young men would have only focused on recording. Although the rewards were great if you were successful, it was a long and difficult road, with minimal guarantees. The hip-hop world, like most creative industries, is full of experienced executives who often take advantage of new artists. This kid was brighter than most, and wise beyond his 18 years. He wanted the whole enchilada.

"I taught myself how to engineer music," he said. "I came to the conclusion that I would avoid the common mistake most artists make. I wanted to control my destiny. *On my terms."*

This kind of foresight is typically reserved for someone who had lived a little more life; Arthit did not have the benefit of experience.

He had gone from a teen to an inmate in a very short span of time.

It was remarkable that he was capable of such vision.

"Do you like rap?" he asked me.

Truth be told, I am not a huge rap fan, other than older hip-hop, but I wanted to encourage him. "I like some of it," I said truthfully. We listened to one of his songs. I looked in the rearview mirror and he was smiling. Not with a boastful, or even a proud look, he was simply jamming to his own music, oblivious.

Clearly, this was his thing, *his* creation, his big idea that came to fruition. He didn't need anyone's approval, especially not mine. He just wanted to share a small part of his dream with me, right there in the car. It was no more complicated than that.

Arthit kept searching for the perfect song. He would cue up a track, then stop, as if it was critically important to show me the best example of his work. Finally arriving on *the* song, he played it, closed his eyes, and sat back and grooved.

Despite the decades of difference between us, I could tell the song was good. It was smooth and flowed, but had an edge to it. Well engineered, with a good beat and transition between the music and the lyrics. I found myself tapping on my steering wheel as we listened.

"Now I'm on all platforms," he told me. Again, his statement didn't have a boastful tone. Instead, he was proud of his accomplishment, and wanted to share his art with me. I felt honored and inspired.

Even beyond his musical talent, what I found truly impressive was his financial strategy. At only 18 years old, with minimal business experience, this teenager had figured out that if you own the rights to your music, you get to keep the bounty. He studied the mechanics of the music industry. He educated himself on how it worked, who made the money and what direction the cash flowed. He then created a game plan and executed it from start to finish, the engineering, production and distribution. By starting his own record label, he would own 100% of the rights to his music.

"I'm really proud of what I've done," he said honestly. "But starting my record label gave me the most satisfaction. Everybody deserves a chance. My two big dreams are to put my mother in a mansion, and give other kids an opportunity I didn't have. A way out."

His work now included signing new artists, and even producing other rapper's music. Best of all, he said he didn't care what anyone's background was, he wanted to give other aspiring musicians from challenging environments a break. This was his way of giving back, and was reflective of the darkest days in his life.

This future music mogul was on a roll and I certainly wasn't going to slow him down. For the first time in his life, Arthit told me, he was earning a decent living, doing what he genuinely loved to do. So much so that he now was taking care of his mom, paying her rent for the past year and about to put a deposit down for her first house.

"I want to watch her walk into her new place. That has been a major goal of mine for a long time," he said excitedly, with a smile. Payback. That's what it is. For all the support and love she gave me. I wasn't the easiest kid when I was younger." He laughed when he said this. It was endearing and honest. "You feel me?" he asked again.

"I feel you," I replied, again, a little unsure of my response.

"You know something? I almost killed her," he confessed. "What? My God, why?" I asked.

"Oh no, not like that," he chuckled. "When I was born. She almost died giving birth to me! You feel me?"

I was confused. The generational gap in my 50-something age was showing big-time, and I was in uncharted territory. Should I keep saying 'Sure' or try and be "hep" and reply, 'I feel you'? Or just nod my head? Give him a thumbs-up? I opted for consistency, and varied my yes response in different ways: Yep, makes sense, sure, of course. Needless to say, I was feeling very uncool.

"Mom chose me," he said. "They had to resuscitate her when I was born. You feel me?"

"That is crazy. You both are lucky! You must have a super strong bond?" I replied, encouraging him further.

He continued with his childhood account, speaking like he was an old soul. "My mom's a strong woman. She was strict with me, and I rebelled. You know, I resented her when I was going through that tough part of my life. Now I appreciate her, and I understand what she was trying to do. It has made me a stronger man. She was always there for me, even in my darkest times."

Arthit became contemplative, and he stopped talking. I looked back at him, and he was glancing out the window, deep in thought. This young adult had been through a lot of challenges, more than any person should have, and was likely reflecting on how important this maternal influence had been in his recovery.

As the conversation dwindled, we drove in the darkness, his music the only sound in the car. The musician closed his eyes again, content. We exited the freeway and I pulled up to his mom's house. "Thanks for sharing your music and story with me Arthit," I replied quietly.

"Dream big, work hard, get better," he said philosophically. "Peace."

And with that, he was gone.

It was a special moment, shared between two strangers who had nothing in common, except music. So moved by our conversation, I stopped the car and pulled out my notebook and jotted down a few things I wanted to think more about.

• Change doesn't happen in the comfort zone. Instead, complacency breeds when things are easy.

• A negative environment can crush the strongest of people. What's the deciding difference between someone who uses a challenging situation as a motivator and one who succumbs to its constraints?

• Pain can be used as a tool.

• Is resiliency learned, developed or inherent in the individual?

I realized that most of us, myself included, are guilty of rationalizing why we can't get started, or more importantly, why we don't try. Fear of failure is common. Similarly, fear of the unknown, success, inadequacy, vulnerability, uncertainty, rejection, missing out, change, losing control, being judged, getting hurt, and the fear of risk are all powerful, but self-defeating emotions that prevent us from being fulfilled.

In the light of Arthit's remarkable story, I looked at my own life, and realized I was guilty of my own limiting thoughts, and struggled with these same fears every day. The negative voices were sometimes loud, and at times I listened to them, embraced them, made them part of who I am.

In spite of my shortcomings, I am an optimist by nature. Like Arthit, I believe anything is possible if you put your mind to it, and are willing to put in the necessary hard work. This form of blind faith is necessary to overcome great obstacles. So, what is the difference between those that do succeed, like Arthit, and those who simply talk about it? What allows people to explore new territories, jump off the proverbial cliff, and reshape their lives?

Mindset, plain and simple. It is all about attitude. Do you feel me?

Peace, Arthit. You are a rare soul and I was grateful to have seen how brightly you shone.

MISHAPS

It was impossible to work in this industry and not see a fair amount of adversity. Some of these misadventures were due to driver error, but most involved interaction with my riders. It still makes me laugh to think of all the mishaps I had over the years. Some were memorable and lighthearted, others made me stop and contemplate life. Almost all had an element of theatrics to them.

The inherent nature of human beings, with all our blunders, mistakes, oversights and bungles, was always at play. It was good fun a majority of the time, but every once in a while, it infuriated me. Still, if I'm being honest, I loved every minute of it.

When people ask me about my experiences as a driver, I usually sum it up in a sentence: I have seen almost everything imaginable in my car. Wild, scary, bizarre and unthinkable. After tens of thousands of passengers, I have witnessed things you would not believe, and a few that I cannot mention. In the end, it was all about people, plain and simple.

A KISS FROM A PASSENGER

*"When my date takes me home and kisses me goodnight, if I
don't hear the philharmonic in my head, I dump him."*
-Rose Morgan, The Mirror Has Two Faces

Passengers occasionally get into the wrong rideshare car. It happens most often when the bar closes and everyone has had too much to drink.

I once picked up a rider, confirmed his name was Ryan, then realized after driving away his name was Brian. Needless to say, I received an irate call from the correct Lyft driver, who gave me a tongue lashing. It's a rookie mistake made mostly by evening drivers.

Another incident, that ended quite differently, happened in the full light of day: 4:00 pm, at the Westfield Valley Fair Mall on Stevens Creek Boulevard. Pickups at malls are frequent, consisting primarily of employees, tourists, and fashionable locals. Pulling my Toyota Prius to the back side of the complex, I parked and absorbed myself in emails until "James" arrived.

The sudden opening of the passenger door startled me, and three high end shopping bags dropped into the back seat. The front passenger door then opened, and a baby-blue Kate Spade purse suddenly appeared on my front seat. Who was this mystery shopper? My curiosity was piqued, as these items were unusual for someone named James.

The owner in question was a stylish Asian girl in her mid-to-late twenties. Dressed smartly in a short black dress and heels that accentuated her long legs and athletic figure, she had obviously spent some time putting her outfit together. Her dark hair was neatly tucked in a ponytail, highlighting her sharp cheekbones and flawless makeup. Bright red lipstick completed the look that, of course, matched her perfectly manicured nails. Needless to say, she personified a model, or at the very least, a fashionista.

The girl's mannerisms were both assertive and deliberate, validation that she had gone through this same procedure many times before. Sitting down into the passenger seat with her back to me, she swung her legs delicately into the car, turned to face me, eyes closed, scarlet lips pursed. She leaned in my direction, apparently ready for an obligatory hello kiss.

With an ear-to-ear smirk on my face, I leaned back a bit and waited to see if she would open her eyes. As she continued her forward motion, my chivalrous instincts took over and I had to interrupt the amorous gesture.

"Hello, a ride for James?" I said, very amused.

She abruptly stopped, opening her eyes. We froze in time for a moment, staring at each other just inches apart, much too close for strangers who had technically not yet met. It was pure comedy, at least for me.

The startled girl went through two quick emotions, both extreme and animated. The first was confusion, obviously not recognizing the voice and the face staring point-blank at her. I can only describe the second expression as terror. Her eyes got wide and the blood drained from her face. She turned about three shades of white. Casper-the-Ghost white.

"Oh my God, I am so sorry!" she said, totally flustered, her voice cracking.

"I'm assuming you are not James?" I said laughing.

"Oh my God," she repeated, "I am so embarrassed. I thought you were my boyfriend! I am really sorry."

"No worries," I replied laughing. "It could happen to anyone."

"No, I am really sorry!" she exclaimed.

"It's no big deal" I said calmly, trying to reassure her.

She pulled back and fumbled for her purse and, in her disoriented state, managed to flip it entirely on the floor. Frantically picking up the contents, she then crammed them into her bag with fast-forward speed, her frustration building. She reached for the door handle and missed it completely, managing to grab neither door nor handle, her body jolting forward awkwardly with the motion. Clearly used to being in control, this poor girl was blatantly not so at that moment.

I looked away to give her a moment to compose herself and noticed another Prius had pulled up next to us, identical to the color and year of my car. At the helm was a handsome driver wearing dark, wire-rimmed Ray-Bans. Looking cool and collected, he could have been an ad for GQ magazine. His window was open and directly facing mine, his arm resting casually on the top of his door. He was grinning like a Cheshire cat.

"How long have you been sitting here?" I asked curiously.

"Long enough to be entertained," he replied, laughing.

I looked back at the girl who now sheepishly stared at her boyfriend and turned even whiter, if that was possible. He looked at my lighted Lyft app, then at her, and broke out in full laughter.

"If you don't take her, I will," I said, adding to the moment of levity.

He paused for a beat and said, "Nah, you can keep her."

She shot him the infamous "evil eye" that only girlfriends and wives can administer to their partners. She apologized again, grabbed her arsenal of bags, and quickly jumped out of the car.

"Have a good day," I said to her boyfriend.

He winked at me and replied, "You too!"

As someone who transports strangers, I've learned the importance of acting professionally. Passengers rely on you, and quickly establishing trust is imperative. There's also a fine line between having a little fun and being a creepy driver. Good rideshare drivers can differentiate between the two.

All of this ran through my mind as I watched the two lovebirds pull away. Her arms were waving in an animated explanation while Mister GQ laughed hysterically. I would have paid money to hear their conversation on the way home.

Real James showed up for his ride a few minutes later and I drove him to his destination with a permanent smile on my face. It lasted the rest of the day.

A kiss is one of life's greatest pleasures. However, looking before you kiss someone is always well-advised.

TECHNOLOGY CAN KILL

"By all means, move at a glacial pace. You know how that thrills me."
-Miranda Priestly, The Devil Wears Prada

Technology is like a razor-sharp chef knife. If used correctly, it makes the job easier. If not, the consequences are severe. The Silicon Valley work ethic is fierce and competitive, and if you are lucky enough to run in this world, you are on the cutting edge of innovation. There have been more advancements, new ideas, and technology progress in this industry than anywhere else in the entire world.

If you're like me, you take technology for granted. You assume it's going to work until it doesn't, and it does 99% of the time. The software on your iPhone updates automatically. Your laptop supports the latest version of that new video game you play with your friends online. The Lyft app you just downloaded allows you to get a ride anywhere in your area. You come home, put your pajamas on, pour a glass of wine, and stream new movies from your couch.

The list of ways we rely on technology is endless. But have you ever stopped to consider the toll all this progress and stability takes on the workers? Bay Area locals like Tesla, PayPal and Apple have rigorous work schedules—I know, I've picked up countless employees late at night who were so exhausted they could barely manage a conversation.

What does an Uber-stressful (pardon the pun) environment do to an employee over time? I can't answer this question directly. However, I can attest to the survival mentality it creates, as evidenced in a trip that originated at the headquarters of one of the most recognizable companies in the world. Technology didn't *actually* kill anybody in this story, but it certainly could have. The ride in question made me question working for a company that strategically manufactures so much pressure on its employees, they would sacrifice their own safety to meet expectations.

The call request I received was an unusual one. For starters, it took place during the day, shortly after lunch. Most of my drives were primarily in the evening. Even stranger, though, was that the entity booking the ride was *Google itself.* Typically, a rideshare request is associated with a single person and includes the passenger's name and photo. In the tens of thousands of rides I've given, I can't remember a single other one that had no photo and personal name, only the company name and address of the pickup.

Regardless, I entered the vast Mountain View property and navigated through the perfectly groomed landscape. It was an impressive sight. Googleplex is massively large, with a multitude of buildings, most no higher than two stories. The grounds cover eighty acres and contain seven million feet of office space. Additionally, there are many activities employees have access to when they need a break from their projects or simply want to relax.

Side note: there is a longstanding debate as to whether these perks were designed for pure enjoyment and creative inspiration, or to emotionally captivate employees to stay longer at work.

Google offers ping-pong and pinball tables, basketball courts, soccer fields, tennis courts and workout fields, and more couches than you have ever seen in one place. There are showers, should you find yourself perspiring from the rough presentation you just delivered.

And bicycles.

The first thing you notice are the multi-colored bicycles. There are wheels everywhere, all riding in perfect orchestration. These unlocked bikes, accessible at every corner, allow employees to whisk themselves from meeting to meeting, to lunch, or wherever they want to go. I have also seen them as far as five miles from the campus—the cycle clean-up crew must have a GPS tracker.

The second thing you realize is just how many employees there are at Google. Waves of people, of every ethnicity, walking, talking and collaborating. Some are on electronic skateboards. Others are getting a midday jog in. All have security badges around their necks, giving them access to creative workspaces all over the property. Navigating through the grounds is intimidating, I had to be careful not to hit anyone!

Did I mention employees also have access to on-site professional chefs, free cooking classes, weight rooms, yoga studios, massage therapists and decompression capsules? Sorry, I digress. My mind must have wandered, as I'm writing this in the closet-sized office in my house.

Back to the ride.

My expectation was to meet a twenty-something Google employee. As I pulled in front of building Five, an on-campus Emergency Medical Technician greeted me instead. As he casually walked up to my half-rolled-down passenger window, my first thought was that there was a medical emergency, and he was going to tell me to move.

"Hi, there. I'm a Lyft driver. Is this a good place to pick someone up?" I asked.

"No, we called you. Can you take an employee to emergency?" he asked, void of any expression—no smile, no chit-chat.

My mind couldn't grasp what he was requesting. I had taken passengers to their doctors, and dropped a few off at the emergency room, but these were self-directed trips. Never had I taken a rider to an emergency when it was critical. My confusion was surely obvious.

"I'm sorry, what was that?" I asked, perplexed.

He repeated what he'd said, adding the destination. "I need you to take a Google employee to the Palo Alto Medical Center Emergency Room."

I was instantly uncomfortable. "It's not critical, right? I don't really want the liability," I replied, being painfully honest.

"We have a full medical facility here on campus," the EMT replied. "We checked him out, he is fine. However, by law, we have to send him to the emergency room for further evaluation."

At the time, I didn't realize this situation was a big red flag. I would later become more cautious and learn that transporting an emergency patient was *not* worth the risk. On the slight chance that something went wrong during our brief time together, I would have been responsible. However, I was none the wiser at that early stage in my driving career, and reluctantly agreed to take the ride.

Jules was a German employee, tall and lean, wearing jeans and a blue Oxford shirt. Likely here on work assignment, he looked the part of an engineer with his untrimmed beard and disheveled hair. No doubt, another coding genius.

When the EMT brought Jules over to the car, my mouth fell open in horror. His head looked like a mummy, completely wrapped in gauze. Sporadic red spots dotted the white bandage. His face was in even worse shape, a canvas of cuts and scrapes. His lips were split open, his nose a bloody mess, and his forehead bruised and swollen. I was surprised his teeth were intact.

I assumed a person with this much trauma would be subdued and despondent. But Jules was nowhere near dazed and confused. Nope, this star employee was frantically texting on his phone, even as the EMT assisted with getting him into my car. Jules' head remained down, his eyes locked on his electronic pacifier. He seemed unaware and unaffected by the current drama he was at the center of.

He sat down in my back seat, fingers pecking at a blazing speed. No acknowledgement, no pleasantries—just total focus on his phone. I turned around in my seat to greet him, and to find out what happened to this unfortunate soul.

"Oh my God, what happened to you?" I inquired.

He seemed startled to be snapped out of his texting trance. Looking up, he managed a smile typical of someone emotionally involved in a book who gets interrupted by an unsolicited hello.

"Oh, was in an accident," he said, stating the obvious.

"Did you fall?" I asked innocently.

"Crashed, actually. I didn't see the other person. I was riding a bike and heading to lunch. As our paths crossed, we collided and I went face first into the cement," Jules told me matter-of-factly.

"Wow, that's terrible," I said. "How did that happen? Were you looking in the other direction or something?"

"No, I was texting," Jules said even more flatly. It was such a casual statement, as if this type of careless behavior was normal and he couldn't believe it happened to him. After replying, he immediately went back to his phone and started his frantic texting again.

I'm pretty outspoken and don't mind giving people a piece of my mind when justified. However, in this case, my intent wasn't malicious or intrusive. I just felt it necessary to point out the indifference Jules was displaying about the condition he was in.

"Maybe you should give the texting a break?" I asked him tentatively, making sure my comment didn't sound condescending or challenging. "You did just have a serious accident."

He looked up again, unoffended by the question, and answered honestly: "I can't. I have a project deadline and need to get this done." Then he went right back to typing like a madman.

I decided to leave the subject alone. After all, it was *his face, and his decision.*

"I'll get you to the emergency; they'll fix you up. In a few weeks, the only thing bruised will be your ego," I replied, trying to lighten the mood a bit.

He must have finished his message because he took a break from his nonstop texting and said, "Isn't that the worst kind of injury?" We both chuckled.

"Yes, I suppose it is!" I said.

"My face will heal. But the biggest challenge will be going back to work and facing my coworkers. For the next few weeks, I will have to explain what happened and why!" he said, laughing.

I laughed with him and continued to drive the last few miles to the hospital. It was nice to see that he could keep his sense of humor even in such rough shape.

In retrospect, I realized the technology company saved a boatload of money sending Texting Jules to the emergency in a Lyft. I researched the cost of an ambulance ride in San Mateo County. After adding the base rate, mileage fees, and added precautionary medical treatments, especially with a possible head trauma accident, the total transportation cost exceeded $3,500.

Now I'm not a mathematician, so I'll wing it here. $3,500 minus a $10 Lyft ride equals $3,490. That was a significant savings. Insurance would cover this cost, and I was sure Google had premium coverage. Yet, still not bad considering Jules' nose was intact, he was in good spirits, and not in a litigious mood.

After looking back at the bizarre circumstances, it occurred to me that Google should have called an ambulance. They shouldn't have shifted the medical and/or legal responsibility to an underpaid rideshare driver. In my opinion the decision bordered on negligence. Poor form, Google, plain and simple.

It begged the questions: did tech companies have to create a do-or-die mentality, where hitting corporate targets was achieved at all costs? Did employees have to be mutated into neurotic, over-focused, and obsessed Type-A workers, to assure their web search executes at a nanosecond speed? Was the price paid by these workers worth the ticket to the next technology frontier?

I wasn't a CEO in charge of a $982 billion company, yet it seemed obvious to me that if high blood pressure, hypertension, and premature balding was the sacrifice, we needed to reevaluate the equation. Nothing was more important than one's safety and health. Not profitability, or corporate goals, and certainly not a project deadline. It just wasn't a fair exchange. There had to be a better way to structure the technology environment, and still deliver results.

The hidden cost of technology could be a killer.

THE DUDE

"I'm divorcing a professor-turned-writer-turned-blogger with the libido of a 13-year-old and two published books to his credit."
-Mercedes Tainot, Larry Crowne

He liked to use the word "dude." No, he used "dude" in nearly every sentence. *Dude,* thanks for picking me up. *Dude*, I'm kinda messed up. You're so right, *dude*! His casual attitude matched the way he rolled with his life—reactively.

"Where are you headed?" I asked.

"To Santana Row to see this girl, but I'm not really into it," he said. "Chicks are whack," he added nonchalantly.

"So why are you going?" I inquired.

He paused then said, "Well, it's late, what else am I going to do," as if there were no other choices in the world.

On the late-night girl hunt, I surmised. Sleep would have been a better option.

Mark was a smart, gregarious, good-looking 24-year old on the prowl. Picking him up at the Los Gatos Bar and Grill, it was clear he had consumed a few cocktails. This drinking establishment was known for attracting a young crowd that liked to dance and party. His face had the telltale beet-red alcohol flush.

At first, I worried he was over the top, but to my surprise he was happy—buzzed, but not drunk, and talkative! This was an ideal passenger for an Uber driver who enjoyed a conversation.

"Dude, I am in so much trouble," Mark offered to start the discussion.

"My girlfriend is livid with me and I don't know what to do."

Doing rideshare requires a psychologist's ear, so I obliged and listened. Not that I could get a word in anyway. He spoke like a whirling dervish, a hundred miles a minute without pausing, and continued this stream of consciousness without missing a beat.

"My girlfriend, well she's not really my girlfriend, but she kind of is, we have gone out for a few months now and she found an earring in my bed!" he said, obviously distraught.

"What did you tell her?" I asked.

"Me and some buddies took a trip to Las Vegas a couple of weeks ago, for a bachelor party. I told her that there was a stripper, and that 'somehow' her earring must have accidentally fallen into my suitcase. Dude, does that fly?" he asked innocently.

I started laughing hysterically, and he laughed in turn.

"Oh no!" he screamed. "I knew it! What should I have told her?" He kept shouting without waiting for a response.

I gave it a bit of thought and then offered this not-so-sage advice. "I would have told her you didn't know. You were having a party at your house the other night, and one of your buddies hooked up with this gal. You slept on the couch and let them sleep in your bed. The earring was hers."

I was trying to give Mark an excuse, and really didn't want to know if he was the one who actually got together with her.

"Dude, why didn't I think of that? I should have taken this Uber a week ago!" he proclaimed, then calmed down and got strangely quiet. I wondered if Mark felt guilty and was perhaps having a moment of self-reflection. He seemed like a caring guy with a good heart, but conflicted, losing an ongoing battle with his libido. In my opinion, he was simply immature, and had no business having a girlfriend, or even a "kind of" girlfriend.

"Dude, I come from a good family and my parents are awesome. I had a nice upbringing," he stated out of the blue, as if reading my mind.

I was going to offer a comment about morality, but opted to let him continue.

"Did you know I am only half Asian?" he asked and continued without needing a confirmation, naturally. "I am Japanese and Mexican. My mom is totally chill, but my dad is traditional Japanese."

"Old-school Japanese?" I asked.

Mark replied, "Yes, kind of like that. More uptight than my mom, but very loving."

Ah, so that's where the guilt came in.

"Oh man, my dad would be so ashamed if he knew I was out looking for women," the young man admitted honestly.

He stopped talking for a minute or so, seemingly contemplating this mental roadblock that threatened to thwart the evening's plans. However, as fast as the thought entered, it appeared to exit. Likely his libido jabbing him in the ribs—or more likely another bodily region. I felt like I was watching one of those cartoons where the angel is talking reasonable in one ear, but the little devil is whispering dirty deeds in the other. It was easy to guess who won in the end.

Pulling up to the bar in Santana Row, and wishing Mark good luck, I thought that was the last I would see of him. I pulled around the corner, shut my phone off, and parked for a few minutes to take a break. Ten minutes later, after turning on my app, another ride request came in. Lo and behold, it was Mark.

I spun back around to where I'd left him. As he got in, I asked, "The girl didn't work out?"

"Dude, I never got in. The bouncer said I was too drunk! What an asshole! I couldn't believe he wouldn't let me in. Dude, can you believe that?" he exclaimed.

I laughed quietly to myself, told him it was for the better, that he really wasn't into the girl anyway, and would feel better in the morning. The last part obviously was not true, as he would feel plenty of pain in the morning.

Mark and I continued to chat, or rather, he talked and I mostly listened, until I dropped him off. He seemed tired, frustrated, and was coming down from a not-so-eventful night. However, I knew he was better off, having narrowly missed a morning after of regret, more guilt and an even worse hangover.

Wishing him well for the second time, I told him I enjoyed meeting him and appreciated our conversation. He thanked me at least six times.

"Dude, thanks so much for talking to me. Peace," he said, his last comment.

I assumed Mark was a good-natured guy who acted badly, a

youngster with his moral compass askew. We have all been single and twenty-four before. At that age, moderation is not usually a priority. He was so honest and self-effacing, I felt genuine empathy for the kid.

Regardless of his blurred ethics, it was nice to have shared a genuine connection with him. Characters like Mark made late night driving a little more bearable and the rides seem shorter.

FISH OUT OF WATER

"She'll make ya rich, or she'll feed ya to the fishes.
If she wants to dance, sonny boy, you've got to follow her lead."
-Scully, Summer Rental

I had never given much thought to what mermaids eat. If I had to guess, I would have said smaller fish, coral, or maybe plankton. A burger and fries? Definitely *not* on my list of possibilities, but I learned something new in this job every day.

The creature I encountered that night was bright green, almost shiny, with mirrored scales that extended to her fin-like tail. Her beautiful mane was neatly coiffed in a bun on the top of her head. The curve of her hips turned majestically and led into a long torso. Bright blue-green eyes gleamed like intense burning opals.

Oh, but the sea-maid was angry. Even from afar, I could feel the tension, every muscle of her rigid body taught and inflexible. She had a fury about her that made a sane person want to keep a safe distance. In her current state, no man in his right mind dared cross her path.

She was ravenous, rapidly consuming her prey. Angrily stabbing bits of charcoal animal flesh and shoving them greedily into her mouth, as if on a carnivorous mission to gluttony. Clearly, her last meal had been days ago.

I approached the siren with caution, careful not to upset her aggressive eating ritual. I had heard this particular aquatic animal could be volatile, even vicious, if threatened or agitated. It was imperative that I approach her with caution. Besides, I didn't want to get lured in by an enchanted spell.

Was I on a treacherous voyage in search of mythological sea creatures? A distant European shore in search of treasure? Perhaps an exploratory research project in the far reaches of Greece? Of course not, sailing was not my muse. I was a Lyft driver, pulling up to the newly developed brick building on Railway Boulevard, a block from downtown Campbell, California.

The beautiful maiden in question stood waiting, impulsively eating a burger and seasoned fries out of a Styrofoam container when I greeted her.

The time was Halloween night of 2018, a few minutes before 1:00 a.m. The destination was a low-budget motel. The number of take-out containers the mermaid was holding: two.

Strangely, she didn't swim to my car, she walked. When she got in, the first thing I noticed was the green and silver glitter accenting her angular cheekbones and soft face. Oddly, she didn't smell like the ocean; her lavender scent engulfed my car, reminding me of a backyard in spring.

This ladyfish carried a green-scaled purse that balanced precariously on her shoulder without needing to be held, allowing her to do two critical things: Carry her stiletto heels and continue to eat without interruption. It was a wonderful combination of efficiency and grace.

I have a few strict rules for passengers who ride in my car. Alcohol and food are at the top of my banned list. These late-night survival requirements allow my car to stay clean, especially when riders have been drinking. An inebriated person with a messy snack—a burrito or a hot dog adorned with mustard, for example—can ruin a back seat in seconds. However, for obviously riled-up sea creatures I made an exception.

"Aren't you a long way from the sea?" I said, hoping to instigate a conversation and find out why an attractive mermaid was standing outside on Halloween without a chaperone.

"Very funny," she said rather tersely. And just like that, the spell broke and my illusions fell. She was just a young woman in a costume.

Sensing her anger, I treaded lightly. "You look great," I said honestly. She really must have spent a lot of time on her outfit, and it showed.

"Thanks," she said with a smile, seeming to calm down and notice that a stranger was paying her a genuine compliment.

"What's wrong, you seemed upset?" I asked.

"I am *so* pissed!" she answered back, her mood reverting back to its previous state. Not waiting for me to ask why, she continued. "My boyfriend and I went to a party. We met some good friends, had a few drinks, and were having a great time. He had one too many cocktails, and works early in the morning. I was still enjoying myself, so I told him I would meet him at the apartment. He took a Lyft home over an hour ago."

I was a little confused. Why would she have me pick her up this late when her boyfriend was back at their home? Furthermore, a cheap motel seemed inappropriate for a cosmopolitan fish like her—unless there was a problem.

"I don't mean to pry, but did you and your boyfriend have a fight?" I asked.

"You didn't let me finish," she said nicely.

Realizing I had interrupted her, I apologized and let her continue.

"That's our new apartment, where you picked me up. We just moved in a month ago. Our stuff is still in boxes. We hadn't even met my neighbors yet, until tonight!"

"Okay, go on," I said. The plot was thickening.

"After leaving the party, I texted my boyfriend, because I realized that I had forgotten my house keys," she told me. "He texted back, promising he would leave his phone by the bed, so he could let me in when I got home."

"Makes sense," I replied. "Then what happened?"

"After my Lyft driver dropped me off, I buzzed and buzzed but he didn't answer. So I walked to the back of the building to check if his car was still in the carport. It was, so I knew that fu*&er was upstairs. I walked back to the front and continued to call for more than ten minutes! That ass%#le was passed out!"

"Wow, that sucks," I told her.

Meanwhile, while ranting, she continued eating her food at record speed. A bite of hamburger, followed by an immediate french fry, hamburger, fry, hamburger, fry. She continued this cycle while we spoke—mouth full of food, oblivious to manners. I am sure there are still hamburger bits in my car from our conversation.

At this point, I was suppressing the urge to laugh, not wanting to upset her more. The puzzle was starting to make sense. She kept talking.

"So I started screaming from the sidewalk, trying to wake him. The neighbors' lights started coming on. People yelled at me, telling me to be quiet. This went on for another ten minutes!" She paused for another round of hamburger and fries.

"I must have woken the building manager because he came out with his entire family—his wife and two little kids. And I hadn't ever met him!" she shrieked. "I had to explain who I was and what I was doing."

"Your boyfriend was there in the building the entire time?" I asked, showing my support.

"*Yes!* I even threw my shoes at the window!" she exclaimed. "I have been standing outside for an hour...in *this outfit!*"

At this juncture, we both realized how ridiculous the situation was and started laughing.

"Look at me. Just look at me," she said. "Everybody must have thought a crazy person had moved into the building. Nice first impression, right?"

"There was nothing you could do at that stage," I reassured her.

"I am so pissed at him right now," she said with bared teeth, and went right down for another bite.

"So what's the game plan now?" I asked. "Motel?"

"Here's what's going to happen," she said and stopped eating.

From the way her eyes intensified, I knew she was about to deliver a bomb. Her expression morphed from determined to malicious.

"I am going to make him pay, big time," she growled. Her voice dropped a level, and I knew she was dead serious. "I'm heading to the motel. When I get there I'm going to change out of this crazy outfit and call at least three of my friends still at the party. Then, we're going to 7-11 to buy more wine than we can drink."

The fish-woman became ecstatic at this point, arms flailing with enthusiasm. "You know what else we're going to do?" she asked.

I was afraid to ask, by this juncture.

"We're ordering three pizzas and whatever else looks good," she declared in one big breath.

"Sounds like you are going to have some fun," I replied.

She held up a Capital One credit card like she was playing the trump card in Euchre. I quickly made the connection: it was her boyfriend's card. She flashed a mischievous smile.

"I am going to give the pizza delivery guy the biggest tip he has ever gotten. At least $100," she growled. "Wait until my boyfriend wakes up, completely hung over. I can't wait to see his expression when he finds out what he bought last night."

She let out an evil laugh, the kind a classic movie villainess delivers when explaining her plan of mass destruction.

We ended our conversation as she seemed content to focus on the rest of her meal. Her hamburger was gone by then, so she went right back to speed-eating her fries.

My encounter with this mermaid taught me a few valuable lessons.

#1: Don't get drunk and leave your aquatic girlfriend at a party.

#2: Don't piss off a hungry and vindictive mermaid.

#3: Put a spare key under the flower-pot.

NIGHT CREATURES

The night was my time. The roads were quieter, the air cooler, and the people came out to play. Once the work day ended there was electricity, excitement, and anticipation at what the night would bring.

At the start of the evening, passengers were mostly fresh and unaffected. I didn't worry about an incident, or a situation getting out of control. It was mostly happy moods, pre-partying, and getting to where they needed to be.

Driving down an uncrowded freeway late at night was blissful. But as the night progressed, my anxiety inevitably grew. The possibility of someone or something getting out of control became more probable, requiring me to pay attention, stay on guard, and be aware of my surroundings.

In the wee hours of morning, picking up passengers was an iffy proposition. The person getting into your car could be human, or they could be a vampire. You never knew.

TATTOOS AND TESTOSTERONE

*"Like the fat man said, if you have to be careful
not to drink too much,
it's because you're not to be trusted when you do."*
-Gerry Boyle, The Guard

Patrons who need an Uber late at night are usually suburban, drunk, twenty-somethings. Most are appreciative, some make you laugh, and a few fall asleep. Truth be told, any of these scenarios are welcome in comparison to the more sinister, scary experiences I've had.

If you drive in the evening, there's a good chance you will encounter a few undesirable passengers. In fact, a few of my female friends who are rideshare drivers stop firmly after dinner time, not willing to risk getting a car full of obnoxious men, or an aggressive rider who could quickly become dangerous.

I could tell the weather was changing early one Sunday morning as summer was transitioning into fall. There was a cold bite in the air, but despite the temperature, I dressed in my usual outfit: shorts, hoodie, baseball cap, and running shoes. I wanted comfort when putting in some serious road time.

At the end of a long shift, I was weary from the two hundred miles I'd logged during that night. It was 1:30 a.m., my apps were turned off, and I was a few miles from my house.

Despite what any seasoned road warrior says, after eight or more hours behind the wheel, you are simply not a safe driver. In this delirious state, strange things happen. The road blurs, shadows move, and the center divider jumps out at you, causing you to suddenly jerk the wheel to avoid obstacles that are not there.

If you push beyond this point, which obviously isn't prudent, a strange chemical reaction occurs in your body. A last burst of adrenaline hits and you find yourself wired. Those who drive for extended periods know this feeling.

Despite my exhaustion, I had passed my personal threshold and was awake and buzzing. And in spite of my teenage daughter's chiding about my caffeine consumption, I had downed a Red Bull an hour before and the effects had kicked in. In retrospect, I should have continued driving the last few minutes it took to reach the comfort of my bed. However, the allure of extra cash beckoned.

Early morning trips were more profitable. In those hours, Lyft, Uber, and even taxis "surged" their rates, much to the chagrin of those who had no other way home. Picking up a few passengers at this time could quickly add $40 or $50 to your revenue. So I turned my app back on, and found myself muttering the phrase that has proved detrimental on more than one occasion: *One last ride*.

Taking the Almaden Expressway exit off Highway 85 in San Jose, I had to drive by two popular late-night bars: Britannia Arms (The Brit) and Branham Lounge. The Brit was first, and a request came in from there just as I was passing it. After a quick U-turn, I put a smile on my face, and prepared myself for the last passengers of the night.

The strip mall that housed this bar also contained two restaurants that cater to hungry post-drinkers: La Victoria ("La Vic" as locals call it), a popular but mediocre taqueria, and Nick the Greek, an alternative for those not prone to Mexican. In the wee-morning hours, pulling into this parking lot was similar to a driver's education test, only instead of dodging cones, you have to avoid the staggering patrons. People wander everywhere in various states of intoxication.

Oblivious and unconcerned about approaching vehicles, this group consists of three subsets: multitasking kids, walking, eating burritos and looking at their phones simultaneously;

pickled young men with too much testosterone, trying in lame desperation to secure a last-minute date; and affectionate couples discussing the rest of the night's adventures.

I was an equal opportunity driver. As long as you were nice, I would take you anywhere.

San Jose has a huge number of drinking establishments, each with its own unique type of patron. At the risk of stereotyping, and with obvious exceptions, I could usually categorize customers based on the neighborhood. Campbell appealed to different customers than Santana Row, San Jose downtown bar hoppers were distinct from those in Los Gatos, and the East Side crowd was different from Willow Glen.

At that hour, it was also a bit of a crap shoot as to who would be getting into your car, and what condition they were in.

However, this was my hood, the San Jose South. As I drove up to the front door of the Brit, I immediately realized this trip would include three men who were not the usual suspects found in this area. Looking like hard-core bikers, they defined a motley crew. Not your pocket-rocket street-racer type, but the Harley-driving motorcycle-gang kind. Mid-40s, big, heavily muscled, with full-body tattoos, they were an intimidating looking bunch. So much so, the other customers avoided them as they stood in front of the door.

Adorned in gold chains, one of the men wore a sports-team tank top and matching shorts. The second was even more stylish, combining extra-long shorts, high-top shoes, and a white ribbed tank top, often called a 'wife beater' by the politically incorrect. The third guy wore black jeans and a flannel shirt. Mr. Flannel was a bit older than the other two, spoke slower and more deliberately, and was the obvious ringleader.

They kept me waiting while they finished their cigarettes. Unless asked to do so, drivers frowned upon this kind of behavior, as it was obviously disrespectful. They squeezed into my Prius, a residual smoky haze following them. Two of the men got into the back seat and one sat in front, which was another red flag. Many late-night passengers avoided the front seat, finding it too close and personal.

The three immediately started talking to me, while the guy in the front seat uncomfortably slapped my shoulder. "How's it going, man?" he said in a belligerent tone.

I am pretty even-tempered, and like to think my judgement is pretty good. I have also played a fair share of poker, and can assess people quickly. These are also survival instincts you develop driving nights. The vibe I got from these guys immediately put me on guard.

"Good, busy tonight," I said warily.

I could tell they'd had a hard night of drinking. Alcohol affects different people in various ways. Some it makes happy, others sleepy. For a few, drinking generates aggressiveness—which is how these three were acting. More alarming was their strange behavior; I assumed drugs were part of the evening's intake. Their language was crude and offensive, centering on the women they had met and the attributes of each. Neanderthal speech, it extended well beyond a "she was hot" discussion. They tried to engage me.

"You got a wife or girlfriend, dude?" the cretin in the front seat asked without invitation.

"Divorced," I said plainly, trying hard to not get involved in their engaging conversation.

"You fucking like this job?" another asked me.

"It's cool, I guess. I like the flexibility," I said without emotion.

Mr. Flannel was the voice of reason, and could see I wasn't very interested in joining the conversation. "Leave the dude alone, he's trying to drive," he said in an assertive tone. When he spoke, the other guys listened. However, they were plenty liquored and continued their inquiry.

Mr. Cretin in the front seat hit my arm again. "Bet you get a lot of tail doing this job, huh?" he said, then let out a menacing laugh. There was something off about this guy. He was mean-spirited, and his questions weren't simply curious.

This ride wasn't going well. We were heading to East San Jose, and after a quick glance, I saw we still had 15 minutes to go. I didn't feel safe at this point.

Uber and Lyft now have a 911 button on their apps, but this feature had not been added yet. Besides, these three men hadn't yet done anything to threaten me. Even if I did want to abort the mission and stop the ride, my immediate concern would be how to get them out of my car. This would not have been an easy proposition in their impaired condition. I went with the safest option, or so I thought, and continued to placate them while I drove.

Mr. Cretin continued to badger me. "You got kids, driver?" he asked with a wry smile on his face.

Ordinarily, I am more than willing to talk about my children. They are my world. Not with this guy. I was instantly uncomfortable. "Yes, I do," I replied with no further elaboration.

Mr. Cretin didn't like my short reply. Number two, in the back seat, jumped back into the discussion. "Ever had anybody fuck with you?" he barked. I looked in my rearview mirror and saw the smirk on his face.

I didn't like where this conversation was heading. "A few," I said truthfully. "I had a woman once start yelling at me the moment I picked her up. I let her vent for a few minutes, and warned her to stop. She didn't and I had to kick her out of my car."

"You think you could kick us out of your car?" Mr. Cretin asked.

I could tell their questions were a test. They were feeding off each other's drunken (or drug induced) belligerence. I kept my voice monotone and unemotional. I also decided to draw a line in the sand and push back, careful not to come off as antagonistic.

"Had a rider who was tripping in the back seat," I said confidently, watching the cretin's facial expression as I said it. "Got a message telling me I picked up the wrong passenger," I continued. "Said the dude in the back seat had a knife."

"What did you do?" number two asked.

"Tried talking to him and he wouldn't answer me. Ended up threatening him with pepper spray," I said in the most business-as-usual voice I could muster.

"Nah, you didn't," Mr. Cretin said, very surprised.

"Sure did," I said. "I wasn't taking any chances. He mellowed out after that and I got him home."

Mr. Cretin was eyeing me suspiciously. A sane person would have taken that story as a warning, but clearly this was not your average outstanding citizen. He took it as a challenge, an opportunity to see if the line I drew was movable.

I pulled into the street leading to their apartment complex, just off Monterey Boulevard. The ride was almost over, I thought with relief. We drove down a long narrow street lined with cars on both sides. Ordinarily, when I'm heading down these narrow streets, I don't bother to look ahead and see which direction I need to exit. I am more focused on parting pleasantries and ending the ride on a positive note.

This was a different situation. I looked ahead and, to my horror, saw that my headlights exposed the sad truth: I was on a cul-de-sac, a *dead end*. I would have to make a U-turn and go back the way I came.

I stopped the car at the desired address and things got even stranger at this point.

Usually, after getting out of my car, people start walking to their destination. The boys in the back seat got out, but stood outside my door, menacingly close to the car. They both lit cigarettes and started to talk.

I turned to Mr. Cretin and said, "Thanks a lot, appreciate the ride."

He didn't move. He just stared at me with an intensity that was unnerving. His look was either menacing or curious—I couldn't tell which. He began to talk like we were long-time friends, in a much quieter voice than before.

"So where do you live?" he asked.

A little unnerved, I responded vaguely, "Here in San Jose."

At first I thought he was hitting on me. Unsolicited offers don't bother me, it's part of being a night driver. You simply need to have a standard reply. After a few shots of alcohol, many people got bolder. Perhaps Mr. Cretin didn't want to let his buddies know he liked men. However, in this situation, I was definitely uncomfortable. Not because of the advance, but because this guy seemed volatile.

"Why don't you give me your phone number?" he requested, in a tone that was more of a command than a question.

"Rideshare companies don't let us give out our personal number to passengers. It's standard procedure," I said flatly.

"I think you should give me your number anyway," he repeated, with what I could only describe as a *demonic* smile on his face.

"Hey man, ride's over. I have to go make some money," I replied resolutely.

"Just give me your cell number," he demanded, louder this time.

"Look, I'm not going to give you my number. I don't give out my number to riders," I said sternly.

"Why the fuck not?" he yelled.

I'm not sure if I flinched, but it felt like I leaped out of my seat. This lunatic was getting worked up, and I was in an enclosed space with him. This could go from zero to bad in a split second. I've had meth heads in my car before, where the conversation escalated very quickly. It took all my faculties to stay calm, maintain a poker face and keep my voice even.

At least five minutes had elapsed since the ride ended.

"Look, I'm *not* going to give you my number. Why do you want it so badly?" I asked, faking indifference. Truth be told, the adrenaline was pumping and my pulse felt like it was going to explode in my head.

"I'm married and have a small kid. I thought it would be cool if you could hang out with us," he said in a perfectly normal voice.

I sat there dumbfounded for a moment. What kind of request was this? My brain quickly searched in vain for any kind of explanation. Why would someone ask a total stranger to spend time with his family and especially his child? *What the hell did this guy want?*

Then it hit me. This guy was a pervert of the lowest kind. I didn't even want to think of the lascivious possibilities this degenerate had in mind. The hair on the back of my neck immediately stood up and I was instantly creeped out.

I was on a dead-end street at 2:00 a.m. with three drunk and likely drugged-out thugs. Two were standing just outside my car, ready to do who knows what, and one very aggressive pervert was refusing to get out of my car. Wedged in a Prius with psycho.

My options were minimal. I was in a really bad spot, and this asshole knew it. My adrenaline kicked in. I sat straight up, fists clenched, and prepared myself for a confrontation.

Fortunately for me, divine intervention took over—or something like it. A knock sounded on the passenger window, and Mr. Flannel yelled at Mr. Cretin in a voice reserved for overbearing bosses and military leaders, "What the fuck are you doing in there? Get the hell out of the car. Let's go. Now!"

Clearly, the two thugs outside had grown bored and I dodged a figurative and possibly literal bullet.

The cretin flashed me the kind of malevolent smile you see in horror films—menacing and evil, full teeth exposed. Think Hannibal Lecter in *Silence of the Lambs.*

The door slammed and I hit the gas so hard my tires squealed. I flipped a Mario Andretti-like U-turn, and headed back toward the group at an urgent pace. The two guys who had been waiting outside the car now jumped in front of it, blocking my way and not seeming to care whether I ran them over.

Mr. Flannel approached my window and knocked for me to open it. I honestly thought the last thing I was going to see was the muzzle of a gun.

I saw a $20 bill instead.

"Sorry for my friend's behavior. He's wasted out of his mind. This is for your time and hassle," Mr. Flannel said sympathetically.

I grabbed the $20 and hightailed it out of there, drove home, and poured myself a strong pull of whiskey.

Reflecting back, the situation could have escalated badly. Maybe Mr. Cretin was testing me to see how far he could push. Perhaps trying to get me to react aggressively toward him, to justify an assault? I'll never know. What I do know is that if they had wanted to hurt me, there was little I could have done about it. I was fortunate, blessed, or just had dumb luck.

Driving rideshare late at night came with the inherent risks that lie waiting in the shadows of the streets, or in this case, at the bars that contain the creatures of the night. Most of the time you're simply babysitting drunks. But do a thousand rides and you're rolling the dice.

IS THAT PEPPER SPRAY?

"Do you know that it's safer to fly than drive a car?"
-Randy, One Night at McCool's

The threat of pepper spray was as good as using it. Easily accessible, located in the little compartment of my car door, it was always within reach. When the crazies came out to play, when the professional drinkers needed a ride home, when the wasted folk decided to call it a night, it was comforting to know it was there.

For the most part, evening passengers were benign and relatively predictable. Frequently inebriated, happy but loud, they engaged you, made you laugh, and even solicited you to participate in their antics. Dealing with people who had consumed a few cocktails was part of the job description, and I managed according to their condition.

When I drove till last call at the bars, I would also see the seedy side of a city and the creatures that thrived in that urban environment. The patrons I encountered were not limited to millennials out having a good time. I would occasionally rub shoulders with the less fortunate—druggies, prostitutes, homeless, and those who had way too much to drink. Suffice it to say, the nocturnal crowd was a bit more colorful.

I started carrying OC spray (oleoresin capsicum) after reading about the assault by a Taco Bell executive on an Uber driver in Newport Beach. In 2015, an intoxicated man violently attacked a driver after being asked to leave the car. The driver managed to pepper spray his passenger, but not until after the rider pummeled him unmercifully from the back seat. The entire incident went viral on YouTube. Shortly thereafter, the police arrested the fast-food brand manager. He lost his job the following day, was charged and convicted of misdemeanor battery, and received 60 days in jail.

The scene was disturbing, and represented the inherent danger drivers faced when picking up passengers who had been drinking. This was also the first time it occurred to me that driving could be hazardous. My biggest worry up to that point was a passenger passing out or getting sick in the car. After watching the video, safety became a bigger concern.

Despite the potential danger, I continued to work late into the night.

Due to the sheer number of riders we transported, there was an implied risk one assumed as a gig driver, especially in the evening. The greater frequency of people, the higher chance of drama. Night driving was a pretty simple equation. Mix a hundred (or a thousand) passengers with several parts alcohol or other illegal substances, add a fair amount of emotional instability, a dash of aggression, and shake well. This human cocktail had volatile possibilities.

Think about the concept of rideshare. You're picking up strangers at all hours of the night. A random passenger climbs into your car—they could be your grandfather or the next Jeffrey Dahmer. You cross your fingers, hoping this person is not the latter. It's a sobering thought, one you intentionally put out of your mind.

While giving a ride in San Francisco one weekend night, I discovered just how vulnerable drivers were.

It was a Friday night at about 11:30 p.m. and I had slowly made my way from San Jose to San Francisco. When I pulled up to Greg on Market Street, at the edge of the Mission District, he was standing on the corner, hiding his face in his hands. Late-twenties or early thirties, dressed in black jeans and a white shirt, he was spot-on for a candidate having a night out in the city.

My first assumption was he was crying, perhaps from a recent fight or breakup with his partner. I am a compassionate guy and have consoled many riders who have entered my car, distressed or upset.

"Hey Greg, are you okay? Can I help you in any way?" I said when he got into the car, offering him an empathetic ear.

He did not greet or even acknowledge me. Silence is even more awkward in a hybrid car, as there is no motor running when the car is idle. Figuring he didn't want to chat, I left him alone and started the ten-minute trip to his destination.

A couple of minutes into the ride I heard a low, cryptic laugh coming from the back seat. This wasn't just a snicker. It was an evil sound one associated with inhuman creatures in horror movies; it made me instantly nervous. I was used to strange noises from drunk guests when driving, but these sounds fell into the indistinguishable slurring category.

Something was not right.

When a passenger got into your car at night, they were a dark figure. Only the outline of a head was visible, their facial features hidden. Your focus was on the road, so you couldn't see what they were doing. Despite my unease, I chose to ignore the spooky laugh and continued my driving.

I glanced at my phone and noticed a message from the owner of the Lyft account of the ride in progress. I was immediately confused. It was from Greg's account, my current passenger, who had booked the ride.

The text read: "You picked up the wrong person. The guy in your car was waving his hands and had a knife."

I couldn't believe what I was reading. If what it said was true, I was properly fucked. Of course, sometimes people booked rides for other passengers, such as a spouse or close friend. But they always sent me a message, explaining the situation.

In this case, however, I had someone in my back seat that wasn't Greg, despite having confirmed his name when he first got in. More important, this stranger *was in my car*, with a weapon, and *my back was turned.*

A wave of adrenaline shot through my body. I didn't just feel the pulse in my temples, I heard it. Instantly alert, I slowly turned my head sideways to see what Greg was doing, all the while struggling to avoid crashing the car. He didn't seem to notice the text, so I figured I had about ten seconds to decide what to do. Whatever choice I made, I realized with horror, might save or cost me my life.

My mind raced while my body struggled to react. I was conflicted by the debilitating combination of disbelief and panic. I have a cool-under-pressure demeanor, but I had never been put in such a compromising spot, one where my immediate safety was in question. A person couldn't practice for a situation like this, I simply had to rely on instinct.

I consciously focused on my breathing. In threatening circumstances, one doesn't have a lot of time for decisions. Whether it was instinct or simply stupidity, my mind was made up.

"I got this," I said quietly to myself. In a voice louder than normal,

I started talking to Greg aggressively. "Hey buddy, how are you feeling? Talk to me," I said in an impatient tone.

There was no answer.

"Hey! If you don't answer me, you're going to get out of my car!" I said more loudly this time. My left hand was on my door, and I was ready for a quick, parkour-like exit if needed. Still no response from my passenger.

I wasn't asking a third time. Reaching down to my side-door compartment, I very slowly grabbed my pepper spray.

Despite his condition, and what I thought was a covert move, Greg managed to see my shift sideways. He instantly perked up and quickly asked, "What was that?"

"Precaution," I said, in the most authoritative voice I could muster, considering the circumstances.

"That's pepper spray, isn't it?" Greg asked in a concerned tone.

"Yes, and I will use it in a second if I have to!" I said assertively.

"No, no, no! I'm wasted and need to get home," Greg pleaded. "My girlfriend's going to totally kill me!"

Despite Greg's appeal, I still had a potential threat in my car, and felt I had to take control of the escalating situation. By this time, his destination was only a couple of minutes away.

"What's the address we are going to?" I asked, quickly covering my phone with my hand.

Greg easily confirmed the correct address.

"Sit there, don't move, or I use this!" I said sharply, holding the pepper spray canister in the air. Fortunately, I could see his apartment was only a few blocks away. I continued to drive with my left hand on the wheel, pepper spray in my right, half-turned in my seat, one eye on the road, and the other on Greg.

It was the longest two minutes of my life.

We pulled up to his apartment building. Greg apologized profusely, thanked me for the ride, and couldn't get out of my car fast enough. I let out a huge sigh and hung my head on the steering wheel.

I quickly did a mental run-through of the last terrifying ten minutes. What could I have done differently? Even though I had managed to escape unscathed, albeit emotionally scarred, in retrospect, the safer alternative would have been to jump out of the car with the pepper spray and tell Greg to get the hell out— the ride was over. Why hadn't I done the smart thing? For a few dollars I had risked my life, and the thought made me sick to my stomach.

Turning off my Lyft app, I drove the long ride home to San Jose in silence.

That ride changed me. I was still cordial with my passengers, but my friendliness was limited. More guarded, I now looked at each rider skeptically, with more scrutiny. This callousness built up over time, and was a telltale sign that I had overextended my time on the road.

In the end, Greg had done nothing wrong. His behavior was strange, that's all.

My best guess is that a group of friends were partying, Greg became too intoxicated, and one of his buddies ordered a Lyft to get him home. The remaining group decided it would be funny to play a joke on the driver. Needless to say, I failed to find the humor in the prank, assuming that's what it was. The situation could have escalated and been dangerous for either me or Greg.

Because of this ride, and many others where I didn't feel safe, I no longer picked up passengers after 1:00 a.m. Despite increasing fares in the early morning hours it was just not worth the extra money. On the slight chance the implied risk became real during one of those drives, I decided it was better to be safe than sorry. And you'd better believe I kept the pepper spray handy, just in case.

VOICES

"To whom am I speaking with now?"
-Dr. Fletcher, Split

It had been a busy midweek evening driving Lyft, with passengers taking me as far from home as North Berkeley. Unusual for a driver who originates in South San Jose, fifty miles away. I was seven hours in at that point and on my way home for a hot date with Netflix and two fingers of my favorite whiskey.

After receiving a call for a pickup in San Leandro, I worried this new ride might backtrack me to Oakland, or possibly San Francisco, and I was hesitant to accept the request. Until recently, Uber didn't disclose the destination until passengers got into the car and the ride started. Lyft still keeps drivers in the dark, which makes it challenging for drivers to manage their time.

Rent was due on Friday, so I confirmed the ride, crossed my fingers, and conceded to taking this passenger wherever he needed to go.

The pickup was 24 Hour Fitness in San Leandro. This usually meant a short ride, as most people go to a gym located a few miles from their home. Smiling to myself, I took this for a routine trip. It seemed my plan to binge watch *Game of Thrones* was going to work after all.

When I picked up Harold, he didn't look like a seasoned gym

rat. No color-coordinated Under Armor outfit, he sported a mismatched ensemble of black shorts, a red t-shirt and a light green hoodie. Slightly heavier than average and in his mid-twenties, I guessed, he carried an inexpensive gym bag, the kind a 60-year old would bring to his first workout.

It was dark, so once Harold got into the car he was just a shadow in the backseat. I greeted him with a friendly hello, but received a minimal reply. The lack of conversation didn't offend me, as some people prefer to keep to themselves. I left him alone to his thoughts, or whatever occupied him.

Tired and mesmerized by the road, I went into autopilot. Harold didn't need much attention and seemed contented for the moment. Happy to accommodate his quiet mood, I continued to drive, my eyes locked onto the lines on the freeway.

Most passengers use their phones on their trips, especially in the evening. So when I first heard voices coming from the back seat, I didn't give it much thought. He was obviously engrossed in YouTube or streaming a movie. But soon I realized something was amiss, though I couldn't put my finger on what it was.

I snapped out of my road fog, straining to hear the back-and-forth conversation going on behind me. The voices seemed louder than what I normally heard coming from a video. And more real. It sounded almost like there was a group of people in the car, all speaking in distinctly different voices.

Man Voice #1: "How have you been?"

Harold: "Good, been busy. Trying to get some exercise these days."

Female Voice: "It's good that you are keeping yourself healthy."

Harold: "Yes, trying to. It's not easy with work and no car."

Man Voice #2: "What happened to your car?"

Harold: "I don't know, it just stopped the other day in Hayward. Didn't sound good though, maybe a transmission."

Man #2: "That sucks. Transmissions are expensive."

Harold: "Yeah, I hope not. Don't have that kind of cash lying around."

Man Voice #3: "Where are you living these days?"

Harold: "Oakland, by the airport. Living with my mom now, trying to save some money. You know, the Bay Area is expensive."

Man #3: "Don't I know it. I'm working two jobs just to pay the rent for a one-bedroom place."

Man Voice #2: "How about you, Sally, what have you been doing?"
Female Voice: "I'm enrolled in a community college, taking some GE classes."

Man Voice #1: "Where are you headed once you transfer from community college?"

Female Voice: "Maybe Mills College or San Francisco State."

Four distinct voices, including a woman's, were conversing out loud in my back seat. Each one had a completely different tone and dialect. It didn't sound like someone trying to imitate another's voice, nor did the discourse have the recorded sound of a movie. The more I listened to this chat, with all its local references, the more confused I became.

I turned my head slightly to seem less obvious, and glanced in the back seat. To my horror, there was no phone, no lit screen, or electronics of any kind. My heart skipped a beat.

Four different personalities were having a conversation, *and the only one in the backseat was Harold.*

First, I panicked. Anxiety took over, and my eyes blurred. The car seemed to decelerate on its own, and my driving felt sluggish, like slow-motion replay. I prided myself on the ability to control my rides: pace of the conversation, passenger moods, car speed, storytelling, and music. However, having never been in a situation like this before, I was at a serious loss about what to do next.

My mind changed gears and started racing, searching for a possible next move. Pull the car over? He could be dangerous. Talk to him? I was too scared at that point to interrupt the continuing conversation. Tell him to stop? Being aggressive did not seem wise at the moment.

I did absolutely nothing. I continued to drive and kept quiet, hoping that he would either stop or suddenly start laughing, telling me that this was a social experiment for his psychology class. Harold did neither.

Listening to the conversing voices was unnerving. My eyes darted back and forth between the time remaining on my Lyft app and the clock on the dash of my Prius. I knew I needed to keep it together. There were ten minutes left before reaching the destination, another ten minutes of unnerving hell.

The four personalities continued their conversation until we were just exiting the freeway, but the dialogue turned hazy as my brain's inability to absorb the alarming circumstances shut it out—a defense mechanism. Fear can do funny things to you, and it definitely did a number on me for those few terrifying minutes on the freeway.

When we pulled up to Harold's house in North Oakland, he couldn't get out of the car fast enough for me. He fumbled around with his bag and belongings for what seemed like an eternity. Finally, he stepped out of the car and held the door open, looking at me with an expressionless gaze.

"Thanks Brian, have a good night," Harold said matter-of-factly, as if nothing had happened.

"Goodnight?" I replied in a confused question. I breathed deeply. The ordeal was over.

Immediately afterwards, I turned my Lyft app off, drove to an In-n-Out parking lot, parked the car, and tried to make sense of what had just happened.

Questions consumed me. Did I just meet a schizophrenic, or did Harold simply have a demented sense of humor? Was this a cruel joke he would tell his friends about? Was he secretly recording me, and I would find myself on YouTube?

I will never know. I'm just grateful his malicious personality wasn't very talkative that night.

Harold proved the law of averages when driving. Do a thousand rides, and the bulk of the trips would be uneventful and drama-free. On the other hand, it was inevitable that a few passengers would be suspect. The expectation was that these questionable riders were predictable—drunk, angry, sad or rude. There was no way to prepare for a person like Harold, nor was a situation like this anywhere to be found in the rideshare driver's training manual.

I don't pretend to understand mental illness. If Harold did have psychological problems, I wish him the best in his recovery. In the event this was truly a case of multiple personalities, he definitely needed to change his medication.

THE HOOKER AND THE HIGH-SPEED CHASE

"I find myself in the middle of the wire. And I feel the void. And although a wire-walker should never look down...I do.
And it was...
It was beautiful. It was calm and beautiful, and serene, and not-dangerous."
-Philippe Petit, The Walk

After midnight a driver can make, in a few hours, what he normally makes in an entire shift. During those hours I had my share of crappy rides and questionable passengers. There is a whole subculture that operates in a big city when everyone else is asleep. Most of those characters I most definitely didn't want in my car. Best case scenario, someone passed out or got sick. I preferred not to think about the worst.

I'd been driving for more than eight hours, and felt tired and cranky. When I was exhausted, I knew the likelihood of an accident was greater. As fatigue set in my judgement could become impaired. Other vehicles also posed a danger. I always had to pay close attention on my ride home, or it could be my last. This was especially true in San Jose, as many folks were coming home from the bars. I saw countless cars crossing the freeway lines in early-morning, and the margin of error was minimal.

It was Friday at 2:00 a.m.; I received a request in the downtown area, from a guy named John. A common name, it didn't warrant much thought until the irony of it hit me later.

After following the directions on my GPS I arrived at the pickup spot, but my passenger was missing. I called the rider, my patience worn thin by too many miles on the road that night.

"Hey, this is Brian, your driver. Where are you?" I asked irritably. Pleasantries were minimal at this hour.

"Oh, I'm sorry," he told me, not sounding sorry. "I put in the wrong address. I need you to pick up my girlfriend at the Motel 6, First and Brokaw Streets."

I was a big boy. At 2:00 a.m., I knew what a pickup at the Motel 6 meant. If forced to make an educated guess, I would have bet a small fortune that my next passenger would be a dubious one at best. Of course, this fact didn't dissuade me. Fares being much higher at this time, and drivers getting a fixed percentage, I agreed to drive the extra ten minutes down the freeway and pick up this unknown person.

The neighborhood in question was a mix of business contradictions. Located by the San Jose airport, it was on the fringe of a large technology hub which hosted some big companies like Samsung and Cisco. Conversely, one of the seediest motels in San Jose, located a few yards from PayPal, sat next to an all-night McDonald's. There were also two casinos within walking distance. The neighborhood diversity meant the crowd changed drastically when the sun went down.

As I pulled into the second-seamiest motel in the area, I realized right from the get-go that its parking lot was a breeding ground for off-the-grid business dealings. For starters, a group of men dressed in dark hoodies stood by the entrance, busy selling drugs. Not knowing if one of these men booked the ride, I rolled down my window and got propositioned for a sale.

"No, I'm cool, just here for a ride," I said in a relaxed voice, after pointing to my Uber light. "Maybe next time." They all laughed and waved me on. As a seasoned driver at night, I met a variety of people, so a situation like this was not intimidating. I found it was important to be friendly, but assertive.

First question answered. However, my test would get harder.

A circular path ran around the motel, and I was about to pull around back to see if my passenger was waiting for me when I glanced to my right and saw a man screaming in my direction. One of those questionable people I referred to earlier, but not my rider, I gathered. The man was standing next to a beat-up Toyota Camry with a huge dent in the side, like it had been in an accident. Confused, I looked on the other side of my car to see if there was someone else he was screaming at. Unfortunately, no one was there. I quickly realized it was directed at me.

My window was still half-down from my conversation with the pharmaceutical entrepreneurs, and the irate man was aggressively advancing toward my window. After immediately rolling it up to avoid close contact, I was able to get a good look at this handsome man. Describing him as rough would be a compliment. Dirty and disheveled, he had wild eyes that signaled a dangerous kind of crazy. He was missing his two front teeth; the rest were stained black, the corners of his mouth encrusted with some white substance I could only guess at. Perhaps an intimate relationship with a crack pipe.

Why was this man angry with me? I was sure I had never met him, as most of my friends abstained from smoking cocaine. Not wanting anything to do with him, I pulled the car around the building, checking my side mirrors to make sure he was not following me.

In hindsight, cancelling my passenger's ride would have been the smarter option. But as I had driven thousands of evenings in some of the most unsavory locations in the Bay Area, safety didn't cross my mind. Evening drivers were certainly jaded, or at least this one was.

There was an ugliness at night that was hard to explain. The callous mentality one developed driving in the evening was probably similar to that of a vice cop. I got so used to the atrocities, they became routine.

My car wasn't parked for more than a couple of minutes, when one of the motel doors opened. A gaunt brunette started walking intently towards my car. Tina was dressed in jeans, tennis shoes and a pink t-shirt that read: "Princess". The polished look was completed by a thin, zip-up sweatshirt with a fake fur collar.

I managed a quick smile, then looked at her destination: the Berryessa neighborhood of San Jose. Southbound. It was getting late at that point, and I lived in that area of the city. I could get Tina there and head home afterwards.

Tina opened the door and stuck her head in to confirm her name. Glancing in my rearview mirror, I saw my worst fears coming to life. The crackhead with the Camry was quickly approaching from behind.

"Get in the car," I said urgently. This was not the time to worry about politeness.

"What?" she asked, obviously startled by my abruptness.

"Get in the car!" I yelled.

She swiftly popped into the back seat just as we both felt a solid thud from behind, jolting my car forward.

Startled, she exclaimed, "What was that about?"

"Some crackhead gave me a hard time while I was waiting for you," I said anxiously. "Let's get out of here, this area is sketchy."

Quickly pulling my Prius around the other side of the building, we swiftly exited onto Brokaw Avenue. A few hundred yards away, we stopped at a red light under the freeway underpass and waited to turn left onto Route 87 South. There were no other cars around at that hour. I frantically looked in the rearview mirror and saw it again: the Camry was coming at us, *and it was not stopping*. The Toyota accelerated, approaching at rapid speed.

We were about to get hit a second time, and it would be a serious collision. Normally, I didn't curse in front of my riders, but this situation justified it. "Shit, we're going to get hit!" I screamed. I tightened my grip on the steering wheel, and braced for the impact. Then my instincts kicked in and I did what I thought I had to do. "Screw this," I murmured to myself.

Running the red light, I swung my Prius around in a U-turn, tires screeching. Pedal down, I fully accelerated and approached the First Street intersection, which also had a red light. Cars from the adjacent intersection were just beginning to turn. I flicked my lights on and off and honked as we cut two lanes off. Not letting up on the gas, I made another U-turn, and pushed the car as hard as I could. We were now entering the on-ramp to Highway 101, heading north.

"Aren't we headed in the wrong direction?" my passenger asked me rather unemotionally. Her voice startled me. In the chaos, I had forgotten I still had a rider in my car.

Tina's destination was south. But in this strained moment, direction was the least of my concerns. I had a madman behind me, who had purposely run into me, tried a second time, and was attempting a third. I also feared he might have a weapon. I still didn't know why he was chasing me. It didn't matter, I just knew I had to get away. Under those circumstances, I chose to ignore her question.

My right foot stomped on the gas pedal until it reached the floor, increasing my speed as quickly as possible. I prayed for a Highway Patrol officer. We merged into the middle lane quickly—60 mph, 70 mph, and then 80 mph. I lost track of speed, my priority now focused on losing this creep.

It was 2:30 a.m. and the freeway was quiet. Then I saw the headlights. The Camry! It was gaining ground quickly, and there was nothing I could do about it. My mind raced, analyzing all options.

"Call 911!" I screamed at Tina.

"Who is this guy? Why is he following us?" Tina again asked, in a way that could only be described as indifferent. You would assume a woman, or anybody in this situation, would be hysterical. It should have been my first clue that something was amiss.

"I don't fucking know!" I yelled back at her. "He was yelling at me in the parking lot. I don't know who he is."

"911, what's your emergency?" the voice on the other side of Tina's phone asked.

"There's a car chasing us, on Highway 101 North," Tina told the police, her voice unaffected. "What kind of car is it?" she asked me.

"Toyota Camry, white, older, big dent," I answered back, eyes still fixated in my rearview mirror.

Meanwhile, the Camry was gaining on us, only a few feet from my bumper. I considered slamming on my brakes and letting him hit my car, then trying to evade him by taking the next off ramp.

But a possible accident with a rider in the car, combined with the thread of facing a potential weapon, eliminated that idea.

Tina finished the call and said they would send a unit. Not much help at the moment, I thought.

I swerved the vehicle two lanes over to the right, and the Camry immediately followed. I weaved back left to no avail. This repeated again and again, with the same result. Where was that police unit? The Camry followed us for at least five miles. Time was a blur. We were living out a scene from a bad video game, *Grand Uber Turismo.*

Suddenly, just as quickly as he found us, he backed off, took a hard right moving across four lanes, and exited the freeway.

"He's gone!" I yelled to Tina. I glanced back and realized she didn't share my enthusiasm, for some reason. Which was the second red flag regarding my passenger.

Turning off the next exit, waves of adrenaline hit me. My pulse rang in my ears and my hands shook, making it extremely challenging to drive. In spite of my shock, I got back on the freeway going south to take Tina home.

For the next five minutes the car remained eerily quiet, the hum of the hybrid motor the only noticeable sound. My mood was somber, and the last thing I wanted to do was talk. Suddenly, Tina broke the silence.

"Was that the worst ride you have ever had?" she asked, as if making casual conversation about a minor ordeal. As if this was just an average day in her life.

What kind of question was that? We had just gone through a horrific experience, and this woman asks that benign of a question? This was the third clue that irked me about Tina.

I was irritated, and answered in a tone normally reserved for children who ask for something they know they cannot have. "Yes, of course!"

I did not say another word for the rest of the trip, but as I drove the remaining miles, I thought about her question. Had she had such a miserable life that a disturbing scenario like this didn't bother her? Her question also solidified my opinion, that there was more to this car chase than just random chance.

After dropping Tina off, I turned my phone off. Now fully exhausted, my body shut down. My mood went from somber to foul. I was upset at myself for doing this job, and even angrier that I had used poor judgement. More importantly, safety should have come first, above all else.

There was a 24-hour donut shop off Capital Avenue, the major connecting road between Tina's area and my house. When I was stressed or tired, I stopped by the sweet shop for a late-night snack. A dozen donut holes and milk seemed right (ironically, it was always nonfat milk), considering the night's events. As I pulled into the parking lot, two San Jose policemen were leaning against their car. Perfect. I wanted some answers about what just happened.

I walked over and must have startled them. It was pushing 3:30 a.m. by then and one of the cops covered his gun with his right hand, in a protective mode. He saw me watching him.

"Relax," I said to the officer, disregarding civilian protocol. "I am an Uber driver, and just had a 911 call involving a high-speed chase. Can I talk to you about it?"

Realizing I was not a threat, his hand eased off his weapon. "Sure," he said skeptically, and I told him what had happened.

"Where did you pick this girl up again?" he inquired.

"The Motel 6 by the San Jose airport," I replied.

Both cops looked at each other and immediately broke into laughter. I looked at them in amazement, my mood turning from sour to angry. Either they didn't know how poor their sense of humor was, or they didn't care. This driver didn't share their amusement. After what I had just experienced, I wasn't going to tolerate being teased, and honestly didn't care if my attitude violated the normal respect reserved for someone in their position.

"Hey! I don't appreciate you laughing at me. I was just involved in an extremely dangerous chase, and am coming to you for advice. Do you think you could help me?"

The policemen must have realized they were being insensitive and stopped laughing. "I'm sorry this happened, sir, but we see this type of thing almost every night, and especially on weekends," the lead officer said. "That hotel is known for prostitution," he replied flatly. "I have two questions for you."

"Sure," I said.

"Did you get the license plate of the car?" he inquired.

My adrenaline was still working overtime, and my patience was thin. "Did you hear what I said? The guy was chasing me! I didn't slow down to take down his license number. We called the incident in while it was happening, so it's on record," I said tersely.

The lead officer eyed me with an authoritative gaze, but could see I was testy. My answer was too aggressive, especially speaking to a cop in the middle of the night. However, he chose to ignore my frustration.

"Second question. Was she a prostitute?" he asked, already

knowing the answer.

I thought about the question for a moment. I knew she was, but still felt confrontational. "I don't know. I usually don't ask my single female passengers if they're working girls," I said in a deadpan voice, making sure my face remained expressionless. Getting arrested would have been a cherry on this otherwise melted sundae of a night.

"She *was* a hooker. Like I said, that Motel 6 is known for prostitution. You got caught, wrong place, wrong time, wrong passenger," he stated.

I dropped my head in defeat, and thanked them. As I walked back to my car the second officer yelled with a smirk, "Hey! Don't pick up anyone at the Motel 6 after midnight!" Both cops erupted in laughter again. Guess they wanted to remove any doubt that police are unsympathetic.

That evening, I almost quit ridesharing altogether.

After taking a few days off to decompress, I did continue to drive but ended my shifts earlier. I was also more selective about where I picked up my late-night passengers.

Anyone who says that driving for Uber or Lyft at night is safe is sadly misinformed. There was a potential danger in every ride, as I was transporting total strangers. It was part of my job to assume that risk.

What a horrendous ordeal, that night. And the worst part? I forgot my donut holes.

UNDER THE INFLUENCE

Drinks—adult beverages, booze, cocktails, poison, spirits, nightcaps, brewskis, shots and cold ones—are all an integral part of a festive evening out. Riders who have been drinking can be funny, unpredictable, aggressive and messy. Part of a good driver's skill set is managing all of these behaviors. In the end, I became an expert at managing the last one. It was a survival tactic.

Stopping on the freeway after going 70mph so my passenger could get sick? Expert Level. Rolling down the window with my right hand while keeping my left on the steering wheel? Expert Level. Gauging the condition of my rider's wobbly head-roll, to assure no spillage? Expert Level. I was dialed in.

However, the biggest challenge with passengers' alcohol-induced states was the inability to predict what the end result would be. Anything could happen between the bar and their final destination. And even if you got them there safely, you still needed to get them out of your car.

I found myself, more than a few times, in situations where I had no instructions on how to proceed with my inebriated riders. Lyft and Uber don't give you an owner's manual for this. You have to manage on the fly.

SOCCER, SCOTLAND, AND A FEW BEERS

"The Glasgow invention of square-toes shoes was to enable the Glasgow man to get closer to the bar."
-Jack House, aka Mr. Glasgow

Campbell is located in Northern California, wedged between Los Gatos and San Jose, in the shadow of the Santa Cruz mountains. Once a sleepy, blue-collar suburb, the city has become gentrified. This destination spot now has multiple bars, an upscale steak house, *Frost Cupcake Factory,* an extensive farmer's market, and even a Cal-Mex restaurant, whose claim to fame is a very potent cocktail called an Industrial Swirl. I know this firsthand, as I lived in the apartments above those Swirls— for three years during the eatery's infancy. The crowd at this establishment leaned to the younger side, and the patrons like to party hard and late.

Pickups were usually in the downtown area, but this particular ride was off the beaten path at a small local sports bar called *Coach's.* I texted the un-named passenger upon arrival, but did not receive a reply. So I waited a bit, as passengers had five minutes before cancellation.

A Scottish chap, whom I'll call Scotch, emerged a few minutes later, dressed in a European soccer outfit and cleats. Scotch was an enormous man, the size of a rugby forward, with a full reddish beard and a linebacker's frame. I couldn't help noticing the size of his hands. I'm not the largest guy, but he could have easily covered my face with one of his expansive mitts.

He stumbled to my car, a huge bag of gear slouched over his broad shoulders. It looked to carry half his team's equipment *and* the net.

"Throw your bag in the back seat," I said calmly as he looked into my open passenger window. The simple request would prove to be a major challenge, due to Scotch's self-inflicted condition: he had put back a few beers.

Ignoring my words, he managed to get the front passenger door open after several attempts. However, putting himself and his gargantuan bag into the front seat of a Toyota Prius at the same time would pose a problem. In his first attempt, he tried wedging himself and the bag into the passenger seat simultaneously. The bag hit the dash and stopped him immediately, leaving him in a half-sitting, half-standing pose. He backed out of the car, stared at me for a moment, then at the seat, looking for an answer.

I should have helped him then, but the amusing scene unfolding in front of my eyes was mesmerizing. If you have ever watched the physical comedy of Rowan Atkinson as *Mr. Bean*, this scene shared similar antics.

Score: Scotland 0, Home Team 1.

Determined, he jammed the bag into the small area in front of the seat and tried to get in. The upper half of his body made the seat, but his legs now put him in an equally awkward position. Suddenly realizing his spatial concern, Scotch sighed and sat there for a moment, half in, half out of the car, perplexed. This was obviously going to take some analysis. However, he seemed primed for the challenge, so I continued to let him work it out.

Score: Scotland 0, Home Team 2.

After "carefully" surveying the situation, Scotch made his next bold move. He pulled the bag out of the car, dropped it, and plopped himself into the seat with a loud thud. Reaching over to the bag, he attempted to pull it into the car, sideways over his lap. It again hit the dash, at which point he yanked furiously.

If you can picture someone trying to pass through a narrow door with a long pole, then pulling that pole horizontally, both ends hitting the door frame, you will have the general idea. At this point, it was time to issue a Red Card or at least call a timeout.

Score: Scotland 0, Home Team 3.

Despite my amusement, I worried he would damage himself or the inside of my car. "Just leave it. I'll take care of it for you," I said.

Due to frustration, or more likely exhaustion, Scotch finally resigned and dropped the bag back on the ground. It took all my strength to pick up the luggage-sized object, despite my weekly gym workouts. With a huge groan and several curse words thrown in, I hoisted the beast into the back seat. Thank God for those back exercises.

After getting back into the car and a bit of slurred discourse, I realized Scotch hadn't entered his destination when he made his ride request.

"What's the address of your house" I asked.

He grunted and pointed forward, indicating his house was that direction. I assumed this meant it was a few blocks down the road, and he would tell me where to turn. Being in an easygoing mood, I conceded and started to drive. At least we were on our way.

Score: Scotland 1, Home Team 3.

After some distance, I turned to ask Scotch if we were close. To my dismay, my new passenger was slumped over and heavily snoring. I nudged him to no avail. A harder attempt wouldn't wake the sleeping giant. It was time to instigate the delicate combination of a scream and mighty shove, reserved for the drunkest of riders.

"Hey, boss!" I shouted. This did it, and he regained consciousness. "Are we close?" I inquired, lowering my tone.

"Right turn," he grumbled.

I slowly turned the wheel and steered the car down the quiet avenue. Driving for several seconds, I definitely needed more direction. To my chagrin, he was fast asleep again. It was time to bring out the big guns.

Score: Scotland 1, Home Team 4.

A well-placed elbow to his shoulder did the trick. He sat up and stared blindly out the window. I didn't know if this meant he was having trouble focusing or we weren't on the correct street. We drove in confused circles through the neighborhood.

By this time, my frustration was mounting. Streets in Campbell can go for miles, and I was desperate to end this ride and get on to the next. Fortunately for me, my passenger's current state prevented him from noticing my thinning patience.

"Do you see your house?" I asked sternly, my patience growing thinner by the second. There was no answer, just more snoring.

I had reached my limit. "Hey buddy, you have to tell me where we are going!" I said loudly. This startled him awake. Scotch opened his eyes, looked up, and pointed to the right. Amazingly, we managed to find his house.

"About time," I muttered, and let out a frustrated breath. "You're home," I announced as we pulled up to the curb.

Score: Scotland 2, Home Team 4.

The big man looked at me cross-eyed, opened the door, leaned forward and stepped out of the car—all in one motion. It amazed me that he managed to avoid a face plant. He started to walk aimlessly down the sidewalk. At this juncture, the situation was almost laughable. Inching the car forward, I pulled up next to him and rolled down my window.

"You left your bag," I said matter-of-factly.

He looked at me with a blank stare, nothing registering. Scotch had no idea where he was, who I was, or how he got there.

"Your bag is in the back seat," I repeated. He then opened the *front* passenger door and looked at me confused, as if I was playing a trick on him. "Never mind," I muttered, got out of the car, and opened the back door.

Score: Scotland 2, Home Team 5.

Next challenge, how to get his bag out. Reaching down with both hands, I yanked hard, which produced minimal results. After some serious grunting, I was able to slowly shimmy it loose and give it to him. He just stood there, bag clutched in his arms. I turned the big man around, walked him to his front door, and patted him on the shoulder. Swaying back and forth, he reached into his pocket, retrieved his keys, and handed them to me.

I opened the door. However, Scotch didn't move. He looked at me, then at the entrance, then back at me. Never have I seen a man more helpless.

"Go on in, it's your house," I said kindly.

Final Score: Scotland 2, Home Team 6.

Leaving him at his doorway, I reasoned he could sleep on the porch if necessary. No one in their right mind would steal something from someone his size. You know the adage, 'Don't poke the bear?' It surely applied here. Tucking him in was obviously not an option.

I couldn't have carried him if I tried. Besides, you have to draw the line somewhere, and I was late for my next drunk passenger.

Game Over.

ONE MORE COCKTAIL

"First you take a drink, then the drink takes a drink, then the drink takes you."
-F Scott Fitzgerald

As a Lyft driver, I didn't know where passengers were going until they got into the car. This limitation was part of Lyft's software and, until recently, was also a restriction of Uber. If the end of the line was a high foot-traffic area like Mountain View or Palo Alto, the lack of transparency was not a problem, as I could pick up additional passengers along the way. However, it was an income killer if your final stop was the middle of nowhere.

Weekends often involved rides between what I liked to call the Bay Area Trifecta: The Peninsula (14 miles from San Jose), SFO (San Francisco's airport, another 26 miles north), and San Francisco ("The City", 12 miles further north). In general, these longer trips were more desirable, assuming they were in the early part of your shift. If riders took me as far as The City, there was a greater demand for rideshare. San Francisco is only seven miles wide, and a third of the occupants don't have cars—which meant more money in my pocket.

On the other hand, the likelihood of getting a ride back to San Jose was minimal, so I didn't want to stray too far from home as the witching hour approached. Despite my best efforts, as the clock approached midnight, I frequently found myself in distant places, picking up strange people—far from the comfort of my home.

It was summer and a lively Saturday night in downtown San Jose. There were lots of people out having a good time, and the city's hockey team had just won a game at SAP Center. Shark jerseys were everywhere. 11:00 p.m. was prime time for drivers, and extended to 2:00 a.m. when the bars closed and the locals had to go home.

A ride request came in from the Fairmont Hotel, which often meant a trip to San Jose Airport, about ten minutes away. It was 11:15 p.m., still time for my passenger to catch a red-eye flight. I was prepared for a quick trip down the freeway, with plenty of time to get back to the action. Instead, I welcomed two unusual passengers: a beautiful mother and her five-year-old daughter.

 I greeted both of my new riders with a warm hello and chatted quickly with the mom while the sleepy little girl faded on her lap. After starting the ride, I was notified of the bad news: their destination was Morgan Hill. Although Morgan Hill, about twenty-two miles South of San Jose, was a nice place to live, it was a revenue killer for an Uber driver on a busy weekend night. A fare there meant at least thirty minutes of downtime driving back without a passenger.

Despite accepting a ride that would take me so far out of the way, being a parent myself I couldn't refuse such nice people at that hour. After successfully reaching their house, I wished the mom well and drove off, preparing myself for an *uneventful* hour-long, quiet ride back to the crowds. Instead, my Uber app startled me: a pickup five minutes away.

With a quick U-turn I headed to downtown Morgan Hill, a sleepy five-block strip with a mix of nice restaurants, upscale bars and few wine tasting rooms. The M&H Tavern was the exception, a dive bar where young locals went to escape the fluff. I pulled up to the bar, double parked and waited. Then waited some more. After texting the rider, Henry, and not receiving a reply, I decided to call. I got voicemail.

A driver had to wait five minutes for a passenger; after that, the ride was considered a no-show, and you received a paltry $3.75 (Sadly, Uber took 25% of the $5 fee). As I reached for the cancellation button, a very inebriated man staggered out of the bar. Hello, Henry!

"Sorry for making you wait. I have had a few drinks," he admitted.

"No problem," I said, eyeing him to gauge how drunk he actually was. I had a mandatory rule of only picking up passengers who could comfortably walk without help. Henry barely passed it.

"How are you doing?" I asked suspiciously.

"I'm *great!*" Henry professed, his enthusiasm clearly manufactured by the buzz he was feeling. The jury was still out as to his real condition, but I decided the fare was worth the risk of him getting sick.

I started the ride and, to my surprise, Campbell popped up as his destination. The driving gods were obviously throwing me a bone. This would mean a paying customer going back to civilization.

"Where are we going in Campbell?" I asked, as it listed the downtown area as the destination, but didn't specify a place.

"I want to go to the Khartoum Bar," he slurred. It sounded more like "Cartubar."

"Excellent, I know Campbell well," I said happily, and we trucked on down the highway. Within two minutes of leaving the bar, my not-so-sober rider was quiet and passed out, slouched over on my back seat.

I welcomed a quiet ride. It had been a long night already, and listening to Green Day's *Still Breathing* on the radio was perfect for my mellow mood. Taking U.S. 101 north to Highway 85, and then to the 17, I arrived at Henry's destination twenty-eight minutes later.

Pulling up to the bar, I noticed Henry was a snoring mess. In a not-so-quiet tone, I told him that we were there, but didn't receive a reply. I yelled this time, and again did not get an answer. Annoyed, I got out of the car, opened the passenger door, and stared at the lifeless lump in my back seat. This time my unmerciful nudge woke Henry. He sat up, startled, groggy and disoriented. Getting out of the car, he blinked a few times, reality coming into focus. He thanked me in a garbled voice, and stood stationary, just outside my car.

"Where are we?" he asked.

"Khartoum," I said in my most deadpan voice. "You put Campbell as your end point, and told me you wanted to come to this bar."

Henry looked at me, confused, a look I had seen many times from passengers who had woken from a drunken stupor.

"Who are you?" the man asked me.

With a big sigh, I replied, "Your Uber driver!"

"And where am I again?" he asked, just as confused as the first time he asked.

"Campbell. You are in Campbell and we are at Khartoum bar," I responded.

"Campbell? I don't want Campbell. I live in Morgan Hill!" he exclaimed desperately.

"Well, this is where you told me to go," I said in a frustrated tone.

"Can you take me back?" he asked.

Having just driven thirty minutes from the sound of crickets to a town full of partying millennials, there was no chance I was driving him back. A taxi sat idling in front of the bar. "Absolutely not. There's a taxi right there, I'm sure he can take you," I said firmly.

Henry accepted his fate with no contention. He closed the door and swayed towards the taxi. His ride with me, due to the late-night surge, cost him $40. The taxi would cost him at least $50. In total, his drunken mistake would cost him upwards of $100 with tip. I shook my head and quietly laughed to myself. A costly mistake, indeed.

As I silently wished Henry a goodnight, I wondered if he would learn his lesson after such a blunder. We have all had too much to drink and ended up sleeping on a friend's couch. However, waking up in another city not only makes for a rough night, but takes drunkenness to another level. The next time he was out on the town, would Henry have the horse sense to know when he's too drunk, or would he utter the all-too-familiar phrase, 'Bartender, bring me another!' and end up in another state?

Before the thought faded, the phone beckoned me for my next ride. I drove off, to another unknown adventure, and in all likelihood, another impaired passenger.

DRINK AND DITCH

"I'm very drunk and I intend on getting still drunker before this evening is over."
-Rhett Butler, Gone With the Wind

In my opinion, you're a douchebag if you dump a drunk girl in an Uber alone and go back to partying. It's not chivalrous and it certainly isn't safe. Didn't your mom teach you better than that?

Granted, times have changed and no one in their right mind expects men to actually live by the high standards of a gallant medieval knight. Nowadays when we say chivalry's not dead, we're alluding to the fact that there is still a kind of 'gentleman's code' that any decent guy should follow.

I received a call at about 9:30 p.m. on St. Paddy's Day for a pickup from the Continental Bar on South First Street in San Jose. This upcoming section is south of the downtown area, with a variety of clubs, specialty cocktail bars, a jazz club, and new eateries.

Pulling up to this popular drinkery, I scanned the street looking for Ben, my next passenger. I was in a good mood, but my happy face quickly faded as a young man walked towards my car carrying a very wobbly girl. I rolled down my passenger window, and Ben greeted me hurriedly, like he had some unfinished business to get back to. Which surely involved a shot and some green beer.

"This is Katie," he said impatiently. "Can you get her home?"

Katie didn't qualify as a rider I'm comfortable letting into my car. She'd had too many cocktails, could not walk to my car by herself and, as I soon found out, would have trouble forming a comprehensible sentence. Needless to say, her night was very much over.

She was a petite blonde, and even in her state, seemed very friendly. Ben literally poured her into my backseat. I asked her a few questions, where she lived and how she was doing, mainly to gauge if she would get sick in my car. She merrily answered me and giggled to herself, which satisfied my cautious concerns.

I found myself telling Ben I would get her home safely. This irresponsible "friend" waited a total of two seconds, replied, "great" and quickly scurried back into the depths of the bar.

I quickly made a few judgements and assumptions about Ben.

He was obviously more than an acquaintance to Katie, and not some kind stranger paying for her ride. He should have done the right thing and accompanied her. A stand-up guy would not put a female into a stranger's car in her condition. If they were having an argument and he was pissed as hell at her, whatever the reason, then giving her an earful the next day would have been justified.

But not going with her? Total asshole move. Although Uber and Lyft do extensive background checks, pre-screen their drivers, and know the scheduled route, a drunk young woman in a car with a stranger is simply not safe. Period.

Katie's house was about twenty minutes away, and she bobbed and weaved most of the way. Small talk was futile, as she stared at me and said nothing, desperately trying to focus her eyes. My previous evaluation of her soberness had obviously been incorrect.

"Do you need me to pull over so you can get sick?" I asked nervously.

"No, I'm fine," she replied, and giggled some more.

We continued to drive, my eyes constantly in the rearview mirror, watching to see if her condition would get worse.

Five minutes from our destination the car got quiet, and I glanced back to see Katie hunched over, face down, and sound asleep. She looked like she was closely examining my back seat with closed eyes. I was praying she wouldn't have an accident before we reached her home. I pulled up to what the GPS said was her house, and stopped the car.

"Katie, you're home," I said loudly. She didn't answer me. "Hey Katie, we are here!" Yelling this time. Nothing but silence. I sighed, got out of the car and opened her door. Katie didn't stir. I shook her and she finally awoke, startled.

"I am your Uber driver. You're home," I said calmly. She looked at me blankly, hopelessly trying to figure out what was happening. "Can you unhook your seatbelt?" I asked, hoping she would be able to do it herself.

She fumbled with the belt several times, more unsuccessful with each attempt, then looked at me desperately for guidance.

"I'm going to help you, okay?" I asked.

Looking more like her head was on a swivel, she nodded up and down. Unhooking her belt took some dexterity on my part, because her purse was on the latch and she was laying on her purse. I grabbed her by the arms and pulled her dead weight sideways, then removed her purse and released her.

This was a delicate situation. Being an older guy, I wanted to help her, but at the moment, I really didn't know to what extent she wanted my aid. I knew she needed my help, but this was dangerous territory because technically, she wasn't consenting to my offer to help extricate her from my car and get her to her front door. Which, of course, would involve touching her.

But the alternative would have been worse. If my passenger was male, I could easily have left the poor bloke curbside, and not given it a second thought. A female in her condition? She was much too vulnerable. I honestly could not live with myself if I abandoned her. Even so, there was potential for a huge liability in this setting, especially in the current environment of lawsuits and driver assaults.

I had to help her out of my car, at the very least.

Realizing she was loose from her seatbelt, Katie's mind must have told her to get out of the car, but her body and legs had the last say. She flopped out of the car, and suddenly fell forward. Fortunately, I grabbed her shoulders and caught her, narrowly avoiding a face plant and a serious morning-after story. Steadying her, I made sure to keep a tight grip to avoid both of us hitting the ground. Again, I was aware of the dangerously fine line between being a Good Samaritan and litigation.

I looked at her half-opened eyes and said in a calm, modulated voice, "Katie, I'm going to get you to your house, all right?"

"Okay," she said.

Remembering the pinpoint on the map, I pointed to the left and said, "I think one of these two houses is yours."

Katie squinted, turned around, and looked across the street. "No, that is my house," she exclaimed, and started to pull us across to the right side of the street.

Even though I thought otherwise, I obliged her and started to walk her to the other side of the narrow street. It took an eternity to get across, one slow step at a time.

Katie stopped for a moment and looked at me, and in what I guessed was a fleeting moment of clarity, said, "You're a gem."

I smiled uncomfortably, knowing that helping her could get me in big trouble. She began to move forward again, and we started walking up the pathway to the house she had pointed to. Just before reaching the doorstep, she suddenly stopped.

"That's not my house!" she exclaimed.

This, of course, confirmed my suspicions, and we made our way slowly to the next one. We did this for a half-dozen different homes. By this time, I was getting frustrated. Not only was this kind of *help* not in the job manual, it was now costing me money.

Finally, something clicked in her mind. "My house is across the street!" she screamed. I sighed loudly and we backtracked, and began the arduous journey to the *other* side of the street.

One. Slow. Step. At. A. Time.

Reaching our original starting point, we now stood straddling the pathways between two houses.

"Which one is it, Katie?" I asked, exasperation in my voice.

"That one!" she said loudly, pointing at the yellow house in front of us.

When we got to the doorstep, my intent was to leave her there. Releasing my grip, I flinched as Katie immediately fell at a 45-degree angle against the door, all weight on one shoulder, balancing dangerously between upright and the looming ground. I watched her for a moment in this precarious position, unsuccessfully fumbling in her purse for her keys. My mind flashed to those YouTube videos where the person is walking ahead, but their body is leaning backwards. That was poor Katie at the moment.

The angle of support didn't last long. It quickly went from 45 degrees to 35, then to 25. As she started to slowly slide to the ground, I lunged forward and grabbed her again, averting the inevitable crash. She thanked me, and I then experienced the most uncertain moment of the night: she brought her face close to mine and pleaded very quietly, "Please help me."

Two emotions hit me hard, both of them uncomfortable: panic and indecision. I was the deer caught in the headlights. Katie continued to stare at me while I went through my mental calculations. Help her or decline and walk away? What else was I going to do? I was both feet into a situation: a driver, or any stranger, never wants to find himself with an inebriated woman. The optics on this were bad. Very bad.

It took me a few seconds to decide on a plan. I would open the door at record speed, drop her on the floor, shut it quickly, and run to my car like Ken Miles at the Le Mans.

I reluctantly reached into her purse and pulled out her keys. My right arm held her shifting weight, which seemed to have doubled in the last few minutes, upright. The other hand desperately tried to jam the key into the slot. I am also right-handed, which made opening the door a significant challenge. It was an amazing feat.

The door swung open and the living room greeted us, lights on and television blaring. I turned to see a guy about Katie's age lying on the couch, eating from an oversized bowl of popcorn. He looked at me, puzzled, then at Katie, then back at me.

"I'm her Uber driver," I said in a frustrated voice.

To my surprise and extreme irritation, the guy just sat there and took another handful of popcorn. Meanwhile, Katie was leaning full weight against my shoulder, saying something in drunken gibberish that had the word "Uber" in it. I still held the key in my left hand.

In a controlled but assertive voice, raising it a decibel for emphasis, I asked, "Well, can you help me here?"

I had no idea whether the guy on the couch was a roommate or boyfriend, but at that point it really didn't matter. Clearly, he could see I needed help—what was his problem? He finally got his unsympathetic ass off the couch and relieved me of my duties.

Quickly fleeing the scene, I walked back to my car shaking my head in disbelief—content for a good deed done and frustrated at the extra duties involved. I thought refusing to drive past 1:00 a.m. would spare me these kinds of awkward situations. I didn't expect to be called in to save the day, or in this case, the evening, at 9:30 p.m. Maybe it was time to renegotiate my Uber contract.

In retrospect though, I would have done it again in a heartbeat. An unwritten part of the job description was to be helpful and treat people with respect—especially in vulnerable situations like Katie's. That is, assuming you're a nice guy and your mama raised you correctly.

Chivalry isn't dead, it's just been forgotten by most of the current generation. When was the last time you opened the car door for your significant other or one was opened for you? If you are a guy, try it. I bet you will receive a look of surprise and might even get to be a knight for the day. More importantly, it's the right thing to do.

TRUST ME, I'M A PROFESSIONAL! (The Vomit Trough)

"How should I put this delicately? You have a regurgitative reaction to mistruthing."
-Benoit Blanc, Knives Out

One of my primary concerns as a rideshare driver was the cleanliness of my car. Due to the large number of passengers, it was inevitable the car's interior would suffer. This volume increased the wear-and-tear and age of the vehicle, especially if riders snuck food or drink into the back seat—which they did. However, a late-night driver's biggest concern, inarguably, was someone getting sick.

Although a driver had minimal control over someone's "regurgitative reactions," steps could be taken to prevent this mishap. As noted in earlier stories, I had a steadfast rule as it applied to rideshare passengers who had too many drinks: If you can stand on your own accord and walk to my car, I'll take you anywhere. If your friends are holding you up, you're *not* getting into my car. Trust only went so far.

Late one Thursday evening, a very persuasive passenger convinced me to change my mind on this policy.

With my Lyft light glowing, I pulled my Prius up to the front of the Britannia Arms, a popular British pub known for pairing delicious fish and chips with pints of Guinness beer. Scanning the large crowd busy smoking and talking, it didn't take me long to find the culprits. They were standing well away from the other patrons, and for good reason.

I was looking at three men who had obviously been through a hard night of partying. Let me rephrase that: two men and a semi-conscious third who looked so wobbly he could have been driving a bicycle with the axle nuts removed.

This classic weekend scenario was a driver's nightmare, as more sober friends frantically tried to lift a lifeless body off the ground. Visions of projectile liquids spewing inside my pristine interior danced through my head. In retrospect, I should have driven off right then, without so much as a word. Instead, my manners got the best of me and I thought it best to wait and tell them that, due to their friend's condition, the ride was canceled.

I waited for the group to make their way to my car, the two men attempting to raise their unsteady buddy by the arms. Wobbly legs buckled and immediately pitched two of the guys sideways, sending them toward the concrete. I gritted my teeth, waiting for the inevitable crash. At that precise moment, the alcohol god intervened, and took pity on these poor fools as the third guy miraculously caught the falling duo midair. He steadied them and said, "Whoa, I got you Alan," as if Alan could hear him. As it turned out, this hero would also be the silver-tongued salesperson for the group.

Suddenly, cheers went up from the spectators who were clearly enjoying the free entertainment. I watched this slow-motion scene unfold with both amusement and apprehension. Red danger lights were going off in my head. My vision blurred and my ears started ringing with the words, *ABORT THE MISSION! ABORT THE MISSION!*

Seeing the two half-drag Alan to my car, there was no question I was canceling the trip. The last thing I wanted was this guy getting sick in the car. If someone vomits, yaks, spews, blows chunks, hurls, or loses their groceries in your car, professional cleaning was not optional. It cost $250 to remove the obvious mess and subsequent smell. Rideshare companies charged the customer $150, and a driver received reimbursement based on submitted photos. You then had to argue with Lyft or Uber, and they ultimately decided if the mess was as severe as you claimed.

This "vomit analysis" was a losing situation. Both parties had different goals. The rideshare companies wanted to pay less than they should, and the driver wanted compensation for his cleaning cost. If this happened, you were out of pocket $100, *and* your income stopped until you paid a visit to the auto detailer. Definitely not an ideal scenario.

It happened once in my driving career, on New Year's Eve. I certainly didn't want to ruin my near-perfect batting average with these three characters. But, as I knew, being an independent contractor afforded me little control when picking up passengers, canceling the ride being one of those choices. You had to use this option sparingly or the Rideshare God would send you a nasty email, and cancel your driving privileges if abused.

With this in mind, I casually rolled down the window and greeted them in a frustrated voice, "Sorry boys, I can't take you. Your friend there is too drunk. Don't want an accident in my car."

Ken was the leader of the trio. He sauntered up to my car, casually leaned into the window and looked me right in the eyes. "Please don't cancel, we really need to get home," he said in a calm voice that seemed rehearsed.

He must have been a sales rep by trade, as his style was smooth and his voice modulated. Having been in sales most of my life, I could immediately tell he was comfortable hearing the word *no*, and that my objection was simply a green light to negotiate.

He was tall and built like a linebacker, and carried an extra ten pounds around the midsection that still seemed to fit his frame well. If I had to guess, I would bet he was an athlete in college. Blond disheveled hair with an assuring smile completed the confident picture. We all had a best friend like Ken. He could handle his liquor better than you. Ken was the one who always convinced you to have that extra unwanted shot. He was first to defend you in a fight, and the first to lead you into the abyss. Everybody loved Ken.

"It's nothing personal, I just can't take a chance," I told him.

"Look, we're a very short distance away, maybe a mile and a half. Please take us, we really need to get home," he pleaded.

"I'm just not comfortable with that. If he gets sick in my car, I'm done for the night," I told him.

"Do you have bags?" He was assertive, as if he had been through this scene many times before.

"Of course," I replied, and immediately regretted saying it.

Keeping trash bags in a Lyft or Uber car was almost as important as making sure you had gas in your tank. You never knew when you would get a queasy passenger.

"Then I *promise* he won't get sick in your car!" he said with a wry smile.

Thinking for a moment, I paused. Ken was watching me closely. I was the prospect considering the sale, and he was the master salesman about to close the big deal.

"Come on, how can you guarantee that?" I asked.

He then delivered the pivotal phrase: "Trust me, I'm a professional!"

Let's say you were about to buy a new vehicle. If you were teetering on the edge, wrestling between buying your dream car or walking out and saving your hard-earned cash, this phrase kept you in the showroom. Ken knew that. His delivery was really just a setup for his big close.

"Look, if my friend here gets sick in your car, I'll double the cleaning fee Uber will give you."

Aha, so I was right. Ken *did* know the ropes and probably had been through this scenario before. I pondered the situation for a minute, and in a momentary lapse of reason said, "Okay, get in."

The orchestration that transpired next was nothing short of amazing.

Ken dropped in the front passenger seat, indicating that Drunk Alan and the third guy, whom I'll call Ted, should hop in back. The team immediately went into action. Ted poured Drunk Alan into the back seat, while Ken held him upright from the front seat. Ted immediately rolled down both back windows, then assumed responsibility for propping up Drunk Alan. Ted then literally grabbed Drunk Alan by the hair on the back of his head, putting his face out the window. Ken asked me where I kept my plastic bags and before I could even think, I gave him one.

The experts were now in full gear. From the front seat, Ken grabbed the garbage bag, made a fist, and punched a hole just below the top edge of the bag. This was the first step in creating what I'll call the "Vomit Trough." Ted then pulled his drunk friend's head back into the car and pointed it toward Ken, who shoved it through the hole in the bag. Picture a bag linked around the back of your head, with the large opening in front of you. Ted pushed Alan's head down into the receptacle, creating a perfect catchall—a human barf bag.

Drunk Alan was a mess. Eyes rolled back in their sockets, head popping in and out of the bag, rolling around on his shoulders as though on a pivot. Both Ken and Ted kept simultaneously yelling, "Keep your head in the bag! Keep your head in the bag!" in precisely ten-second intervals. Ted violently shoved Alan's head into the vomit tough every time he would come up for air.

While trying to keep my eyes on the road, I couldn't help staring in a state of awe and disbelief. I had never seen anything like this before, executed with such obvious precision. This bizarre process continued until we safely pulled into their neighborhood, ten minutes later.

As we approached their house, I worried that Alan might have missed his target in spite of Ted and Ken's diligence. Spillage in my car would not be good for business. I jumped out of the car while the other two carefully poured Alan on the sidewalk. Alan sat on the curb, as Ken roughly yanked the bag over his head. I inspected the back seat. Surprisingly, not a drop.

"That was truly amazing"" I said, and meant it.

Ken laughed and told me he and Ted were EMTs, and had seen their share of alcohol overdoses. His parting words would resonate with me the rest of the night, "See, I told you I was a professional!"

I nodded my head in affirmation. "You sure are!"

Ken flashed that wry smile again and I pulled back on the road, no harm done, ready for action. I mad misjudged this guy for the shady-salesman type, but he turned out to be anything but that. Not only did he uphold his guarantee of keeping my car clean, but he could build a mean vomit trough. Everybody loved Ken, and now I counted myself in that group as well.

FRAGILE

"The mind is a fragile thing. Takes only the slightest tap to tip it in the wrong direction."
-Professor Charles Xavier, X-Men: Dark Phoenix

Although meeting amusing people was a certainty, it was unavoidable I would also come across those who were having a crummy day. Occasionally, I would come across someone who was in real turmoil. Those were hard trips. They left me feeling raw and emotional, and reminded me that life didn't always distribute the cards fairly.

I had a handful of riders who were really down on their luck. It didn't make for a happy conversation, but their struggles were real and confirmed the full circle of life. If I met a passenger who needed a compassionate ear, I listened and tried to help if possible. A few choice words of encouragement went a long way. We all experienced difficult times, and it sometimes helped to talk to a stranger.

I had decided to work a few hours on a tranquil Christmas Eve. My children were with their mom, and I wanted some mindless activity to distract me from the fact that I was not with my kids. I felt introverted and pensive, not my normal upbeat, optimistic self.

During the December season, driving activity was busy earlier, and got quieter as the night progressed. That evening was no exception. After receiving a ride request in Santa Clara, I instantly recognized Blinky's Can't Say Bar, located a few blocks from Santa Clara University.

Figuring the call was from a college student staying on campus, I casually drove to the site, expecting to meet a twenty-something heading to a holiday frat party. There were two entrances at this tavern, and I stopped briefly at the back door as it was the closest to me. No one was waiting outside so after a couple of minutes I proceeded around the block to the front. Again, no passenger.

Double checking my phone, the Lyft application confirmed my passenger was still there. I sent him a text, which is the standard first step before cancelling. After several minutes, there was still no reply. It was a slow night and I needed the fare, so I dialed the rider - a last resort.

An agitated male voice answered, "Where are you?" with a slight slur, obviously induced by a cocktail or two.

"I have been driving around for five minutes," I replied impatiently. "Where are you?"

"I am around the back," he responded in a gruff voice.

After a deep breath, I spun the car around a second time. As I pulled to the back entrance, my passenger was still nowhere in sight. Agitated at this point, I resolved that the situation was hopeless and was about to leave the parking lot when I heard a yell.

"Hey, I'm over here!" an impatient voice beckoned from behind a car.

I turned around and spotted Carlos standing in the corner of the lot, completely hidden, a considerable distance from the pickup point. My first thought was to cancel the ride. If this guy was in a sour mood, he would surely be disagreeable and difficult. That combination did not make for a pleasant ride. My next thought was an angry one, and I am ashamed to admit how hasty this assumption entered my mind: *What an asshole!*

Fortunately, I overcame my frustration, took another breath, and headed to meet my new occupant. The man had drunk, but he was not sloppy. He easily sat himself in the front seat, which I found unusual, considering how tense the conversation had started. To my surprise, he was not the least bit antagonistic. In fact, his mood was somber, his voice muted.

Carlos was a Hispanic man in his early fifties, stocky with large calloused hands—the kind that come from heavy lifting; construction would be my best guess. He was twenty pounds overweight, much of it carried in his midsection. But his most prominent feature was his eyes: kind and gentle, even at first glance.

My greeting was lukewarm, as I was still simmering a bit from the parking lot incident. "How's it going?" I asked flatly.

"You don't want to know," he said quietly. He lowered his head when he said this, his eyes on the floor.

Having a compassionate ear often comes in handy when ridesharing. Concluding that he likely had an argument with his girlfriend, or a good case of the holiday blues, I told him, "Try me."

He quickly replied, "Trust me, you don't want to know how I am doing. It will really bum you out."

It didn't take much people-reading skills to realize this man was hurting. I was curious, now out of my funk, and felt that a conversation might raise his spirits. On the other hand, I didn't want to invade his privacy if he was too upset and didn't want to talk. I thought I would try one last time. If he declined a third attempt, I would let it alone.

"Look, we have a long drive. I would like to hear what's bothering you," I stated honestly.

"Really?" Carlos asked.

In my experience, middle-aged Hispanic men were not prone to exposing their emotions. For him to want to talk I figured something heavy must be on his mind. I looked directly into his eyes and calmly said, "Of course."

"Tonight is my daughter's anniversary, my mija," he began. He then became very subdued, and I immediately sensed something was terribly wrong. The conversation immediately stopped, and emotions hung in the air like fog. Looking over at him, I could see he was pensively looking out the window.

"Are you okay, Carlos?" I asked with concern.

My voiced must have startled him, as he instantly shifted in his seat. He put his head in his hands and began crying uncontrollably. "Oh my God, mija, why did you do it?" His tears continued for several minutes, while he simultaneously repeated the phrase, "My mija, My mija."

I put a sympathetic hand on his shoulder, trying my best to console him, but I knew it wasn't enough. He began to sob. Not knowing the full story at this point, I felt completely helpless. He was fragile, and seemed broken. We both said nothing, the otherwise silent night filled with the sound of this grown man's raw emotions.

After several minutes, Carlos regained his composure and finally spoke. "This is the one-year anniversary of my baby's death."

Hearing this, I felt as though I was invading his privacy, violating a sacrosanct boundary of some kind. However, also having a daughter, I could imagine how intimate the moment was, how significant this day was to this man, this human being, this father.

"What was her name?" I asked.

"Melaina," Carlos said. "She was an angel. She was so beautiful."
"It's okay, Carlos, tell me about it," I said softly.

He continued, though I'm sure he didn't hear me. "Do you have kids?"

"Yes, I have a fifteen-year-old boy and a seventeen-year-old daughter," I said.

A wave of confusing emotions consumed me as soon as the words left my mouth: embarrassment, guilt and empathy. Although my response was truthful, the flood of raw feelings temporarily blocked any reasoning or understanding. When I did regain my faculties, I felt a sickening sense of privilege.

Fortunately, Carlos didn't notice my obvious pause, or he chose to ignore it. "My baby was sixteen. She had the whole world in front of her," he said sadly.

"What happened?" I asked.

I would soon learn that Melaina took her life exactly a year ago to the day. She had fought depression for years, and digressed into drugs to cope with the inner turmoil she was experiencing.

Carlos also had a 12-year-old son. On this day before Christmas, I was taking him to see his boy and his ex-wife. The three were going to spend the holiday together, to honor the memory of Melaina, the lovely young woman they had all lost.

"You don't understand," he explained desperately, "she was my life! My beautiful baby girl." Dropping his head dejectedly, he started to sob again, harder this time.

"Mija, why didn't you come to me? I would have helped you." He cried for a few more minutes, and we drove in silence until he was able to speak again.

When he seemed ready, I asked, "How are you dealing with all this?"

Carlos thought for a moment before answering me. "Not very well. I have good and bad days, mostly bad. I just try to get through each one."

"That's all you can do," I said. Despite my sincerity, the words sounded blatantly obvious, clichéd, unsympathetic.

Looking out the window, he continued. "I will see my ex-wife and son soon, and I am drunk. What is there to celebrate?" He turned in his seat, faced me, and begged for an answer I was not qualified to give him. "What am I supposed to do? What should I say to them? They are looking to me for strength, and I don't have any left."

Tears welled up in my eyes. It took me a few moments before I was able to answer him. "I am a father, and I can only imagine how terribly difficult this is for you. Your son needs you more than ever now. You need to reassure him, to tell him everything will be fine. Most importantly, he needs to know that you love him very much."

He nodded in agreement.

"You should try to talk to someone who can help you, a professional who deals with this type of loss. It might help," I added. Carlos acknowledged my advice, but the despondent look he gave me was not encouraging. The emotional battle this man was facing was unthinkable.

We finally arrived at the destination, a modest mobile home park in South San Jose. Carlos didn't immediately get out of the car but instead sat silently for a few moments, postponing the inevitable. I again put a hand on his shoulder and told him in the most reassuring voice I could manage, "It will be alright," even though I had no idea what lay in store for him.

Carlos finally opened the passenger door and stood outside my car, thanking me over and over for listening to him. "Be sure and hug your kids," he said and began to walk away. Then he suddenly stopped, and as though needing affirmation, and said, "Melaina, please remember that name. Her name was Melaina."

"I definitely will, Carlos," I replied. My heart genuinely hurt for this man.

Once outside the housing park, I immediately pulled my car to the side of the road. Thinking of my own teenaged children, including a daughter roughly the same age as Melaina, sadness overwhelmed me. Carlos's honesty and heartfelt emotions touched me deeply. Tears began to roll down my cheeks as I emphatically texted my kids, telling them how much I loved them.

The residual damage caused by a traumatic event like this can tear a family apart for generations. The pain they were going through unimaginable. Nobody should ever experience that type of torment, especially a parent.

For most of us, Christmas Eve is a time filled with joy and thankfulness. Yet for others, it is an unwelcome reminder of things missed. This experience was a blatant reminder of the preciousness of life, and also the fragility.

In retrospect, I don't feel like I offered Carlos much solace, and felt hugely inadequate in my efforts. Carlos did not specifically choose me to confide in, to share his inner turmoil. All the same, I felt honored to have shared this experience with him. Although the time we spent together was brief, the memory of his pain will be with me for the rest of my life.

Wherever you are, Melaina, I hope you are now at peace.

Authors Note: If you or someone you know is struggling with depression, please contact the Substance Abuse and Mental Health Service Organization (SAMHSA) at (800) 662-4357. This number is open 24/7, 365 days a year.

IN MY OPINION

Being a rideshare driver gave me a behind-the-scenes look at a fairly new industry. The following chapters are not more stories, but rather some personal insights, tips, and guidelines from my time spent in this business. Although my intent was to offer an opinion, I also felt it was important to provide additional information that develops a better understanding of the industry, and improves rider/driver relationships.

This transportation service that we have all become accustom to is rapidly changing. Drivers are now dealing with a Covid-19 protection, the possible reclassification of driver status to employees, and decreased usage for ridesharing due to Covid-19. The fate of this industry is in jeopardy, and its sustainability is uncertain. As we watch this drama unfold, it will be interesting to see how and if our habits change with it.

WHY I STOPPED DRIVING

Transporting humans around was not as easy as I thought it would be. From 2015 to 2020, I accumulated over 250,000 miles driving for Uber and Lyft, and my attitude at the end of that period was considerably different than it was at the beginning. For a number of reasons—some personal, some outside my control.

When I first started ridesharing, I was optimistic and excited. My patience was long, I accepted all my ride requests, and went out of my way to create the best possible experience for my passengers. Coming from a sales background, making sure the customer was happy was always top of mind.

Working as a driver seemed like an ideal job, and it was in the beginning. The supervision was minimal, my car was my office, and a decent wage was possible. The flexible schedule was what most interested me. I worked when I wanted, for as long as I chose, and met many interesting people.

Now that you've met some of them in this collection of stories, I'm sure you understand why I felt the passengers were the best part of the job. I had the pleasure of meeting some truly unique, funny, and generous passengers. They amazed me, inspired me and made me laugh out loud countless times. We discussed ideas, shared stories, and even cried together. Silicon Valley is full of creative people doing exciting things, and it was fun to pick up the occasional entrepreneur or founder. It was a slice of human nature at its best, for the most part. Not a bad record, considering the approximately 35,000 people that got in and out of my car.

Yet with this kind of volume also comes diversity. Working in a big city like San Jose, and primarily in the evening, exposed me to the occasional dark side of driving. This meant for every ten riders, nine would be cool, and one would be trouble. It was simply a numbers game. Inevitably, I would come across someone who was aggressive, drugged-out, dismissive or dangerous. Despite the unpredictable nature of the job, I continued. In some ways, the uncertainty was alluring.

But when the novelty wore off, the reality of the job set in. I started logging 200 miles a day, and averaging 75 to 100 rides a week, and it took a toll on my body and emotions. It was a grind putting in that many hours in a car, and adding Bay Area traffic to the mix made it that much harder.

As the concept of rideshare was readily adopted, demand grew, and more drivers began to saturate the market. Revenues of the rideshare companies surged. But instead of embracing their independent contractor drivers, and making conditions better, they became self-serving and arrogant. Adding to the complication, Uber announced reduced pricing in late 2015-2016. Consequently, drivers now had to manage more competition *and* lower wages.

I didn't start ridesharing to move the financial needle, it was simply a means to pay the bills or add ancillary income. Uber and Lyft's compensation structure were designed to keep a driver's head just above water, which meant you could never get ahead of the landlord. So if driving was your primary source of income, especially in the Bay Area, you were forced to drive six or seven days a week to satisfy your financial obligations.

In late 2018, drivers began voicing their dissatisfaction with Lyft and Uber's driver redesigned compensation, and I noticed it as well. Subtracting gas, insurance, tires, car washes, maintenance, water & candy (assuming you provided these items) and mileage on your car, left very little extra. Needless to say, I should have been more prudent with my financial analysis.

To put the mileage in perspective, I managed to put over 51,000 miles on my Prius in my first year, ran my first car into the ground, and was well on my way to doing the same to my second vehicle.

Low wages and a competitive culture were not the only reasons I stopped driving. Lack of enthusiasm and safety concerns were my demise, and made the decision to leave the world of ridesharing a bit easier.

If you do anything too long, and it is not your passion, you have a natural tendency to burn out. Driving no longer was fun, and I began to come home weary after every shift. This was the first warning bell that I was not long for the business. In my opinion, rideshare drivers have a limited shelf life.

Drive too many passengers, and the uniqueness of each customer eventually fades. Once I hit that threshold, rides, and therefore riders, simply became another fare. That was not a positive attitude to have when dealing with the public. When the focus stopped being about human interaction, and I am a very social person, my time working for Uber and Lyft was limited. I had walked the line for a long time, and needed a change.

Personal safety also became a concern—initially with my passengers, and then with this craziness called Covid-19. The first was barely manageable, but at least you could spot the problem immediately and deal with it appropriately. The second was a game ender, at least for me.

Every person that got into my car was a potential risk, especially at night. Passengers had been video-taped assaulting their drivers (and vice versa). I faced several situations where I could have gotten hurt, and I like to think of myself as streetwise. However, the two different passengers that pushed me over the edge were the ones who smoked drugs in my backseat. Both turned out to be benign, but could easily have turned volatile.

Driving strangers in a pandemic is scary. I found myself picking up twenty-somethings from garage parties, with no social distancing or masks. A total disregard for safety. This decision was theirs, but when they got into my car, it became my decision whether I would continue to put myself at risk. An asymptomatic but infected rider could get into my car, and I would have had a serious problem. It seemed like a crapshoot to me, and a gamble I didn't want to take.

In the end, the pandemic was the last straw in the ever-growing weight of things I no longer wanted to deal with as a rideshare driver. I stopped driving altogether in May of 2020. I had a great run, met a lot of cool people, and had more crazy driving experiences than I can count.

DRIVER ETIQUETTE

Your driver has a responsibility to get you comfortably and safely to your destination. Politeness is mandatory. If a driver is not cordial, s/he has no business taking on the job in the first place. Additionally, it's not too much to ask for a clean car.

Other than that, don't delude yourself that your driver is required to give you the VIP treatment. He likely drove hundreds of miles that day, and you were one of many passengers. He may have been at the beginning of his shift or you may have been his last ride, so kindly give him the benefit of the doubt. In spite of this, having a good-natured driver makes the experience more enjoyable, just as a friendly passenger makes the ride seem much shorter. It's a reciprocal relationship.

Based on my years as a rideshare driver, I've come up a list of commonly-asked questions regarding what to expect from your driver, with the caveat that the following suggestions are only one humble driver's opinion.

Should the driver load my luggage and bags?

Not technically, but it is good customer service. After all, you are paying for the ride and we, as drivers, are providing you a service. That should include getting out of the car and helping with your suitcases and bags—rain or shine. Any driver who pops his trunk and stays in his car is a lazy-ass, and should not receive a gratuity.

Is it mandatory that my driver converse with me?

I have been asked this question more times than I can count. The short answer is no. Don't get worked up if your driver isn't chatty. Just like there are a wide variety of people and personalities, the same goes for drivers. Yet many passengers told me that they tipped less if their drivers weren't talkative.

Let me ask you a question: If you go to a restaurant and order a meal, is the amount of your tip determined on whether the waiter talked your ear off? I would bet that when the check arrives, your gratuity is the same, assuming you received friendly and efficient service. The same standard should apply to your Uber driver.

Should drivers provide extra goodies?

The cost of water, gum, candy, and other items provided free of charge come directly out of a driver's revenue, so should not be expected. If any of these conveniences are provided, and you use them, make sure to show your appreciation in the form of an appreciative gratuity.

I did a beta test for three months, keeping track of my rides with and without these customer extras. The result? There was no significant change in tipping. So I stopped providing these goodies. What I did find is passengers would leave their empty water bottles and candy wrappers in my car. It made for an easy decision.

Does the rating system matter to drivers?

Drivers and passengers are rated after each ride, 1 star being the worst, and 5 stars being the highest. I had many riders say, "Great ride!" give me 5-stars, and then didn't tip. Truth be told, drivers don't care whether you give us 4 or 5 stars (assuming the ride was favorable), but we do care about a few extra dollars.

Can a driver legally kick me out of the car?

Absolutely. If you are too drunk, disrespectful, or aggressive, we have the right to stop the ride and ask you to leave. We also have a 911 button if we ever feel unsafe. In general, don't be an ogre and you will get taken where you wish.

Do drivers have to accept a ride?

Most of the time. However, occasionally they can get away with politely declining a ride. Let's say a driver has worked ten hours, is near his house, and you're his last trip. If you are catching a red-eye flight an hour away, it is not in the driver's best interest to take that ride. They can't decline trips often, as corporate will suspend their driving privileges if it becomes a habit. A declined ride is unpleasant for passengers, but there will usually be another driver available within minutes.

Should tipping be mandatory?

With a biased perspective, and at the risk of being redundant, I will address this question. Assuming your experience was pleasant, the answer is yes! You were provided a service, and your safety and convenience rested in another's person's hands. If that person did his job well, a small gratuity is justified. Uber and Lyft take a hefty percentage out of each ride. If you're on a budget, tip the minimal amount. If you had a great time and loved your driver, give him a little extra. Not only will it be appreciated, but it's the right thing to do.

PASSENGER ETIQUETTE

There are a few general guidelines that riders should abide by, in addition to paying for the service itself. Be polite, and treat the driver like you would your bartender. Instead of a cocktail, he or she is getting your sorry, drunk-ass home safely, or at the very least, taking you where you need to go.

The following are some questions drivers hear from their passengers, followed by my ever-so-humble opinions. Again, I'm speaking as one former rideshare driver, not the entire industry here.

Can I request music?

Sure thing. However, that doesn't mean you are entitled to connect your personal phone to his car via Bluetooth so you can listen to your favorite hip-hop song at maximum volume. It is the driver's discretion as to what music is played.

Can I bring food into the car with me?

You want to bring your mustard-covered, onion hanging, relish-dripping hot dog into my car? Are you kidding me? Finish your food before you get in, or take your culinary escapades into the next unsuspecting driver's car. This rule also applies to burritos, nachos, tacos and any other small tidbit-filled wrap you are earnestly shoving down your pie hole. Admittedly, I have some strong feelings about this question.

Can I ask my driver to stop for food?

Let me answer with a typical scenario: It is 2:00 a.m., and you and your friends have put away more than your share of Patron shots. You desperately need food to soak up the Mexican rocket fuel you just ingested. In the nicest voice you can muster, making sure you aren't slurring your words, you ask your driver: "Would you mind driving through the Jack-in-the-Box...real quick?"

Do you mean that fast-food joint where the line extends through the parking lot and empties into the street? Where every car is ordering enough food to feed a small village? This extra stop is not a minor concession. Minimally, this detour will take twenty minutes, so you are figuratively taking money out of your driver's pocket.

The initial request is always followed up by, "I'll tip you extra." Translated, this means you will get home, consume 3000 calories of nutritious salt-and-sugar delight, and pass out on your couch, oblivious to the inconvenience you caused your driver. When you wake up at 2:00 p.m. the next day, you will only tip the minimal amount (if at all) because you have a splitting hangover, just saw the credit card tally for the drinks you bought for the group you were with, and are hating life in general.

Let's say I agree to take you through the fast food line and then you have the nerve to start eating your disgusting fried delicacies in my car. This adds insult to injury. Do I stop by your house, unannounced, walk to your bedroom while you are watching Netflix, slide in between you and your partner, fluff a pillow up for myself, pull out my extra-large bag of Nacho Cheese Doritos, and start shoving chips into my mouth, five-at-a-time? Do you feel me?

Here's the skinny: Don't eat on your rideshare. Period. If the driver is nice enough to get you food in the middle of the night, be considerate enough to abstain from grabbing a handful of onion

---

rings or fries and ramming them into your mouth. Besides, the smell of that $ .99 cent taco or burger will linger in the car well after you have retired to your bed. Your driver will have to endure stinging cold as he rides down the freeway with all his windows open, hoping to reduce the stench for the next passenger.

Can I request a ride if I'm intoxicated?

Why the hell is it necessary to drink until you're cross-eyed? Don't you know the likelihood of you hurling greatly increases the more drunk you are?

Please, don't drink so many cocktails that you spew all over my back seat, or best-case scenario, hurl out the window at high speed, thereby adding a slick, new, acid-burning liquid sheen to the paint on his new car. Not that you care at that drunk moment, but this type of accident is an immediate income-killer for your hard-working driver.

Additionally, the seat that you are sitting on is owned by the driver, or more likely, the finance company who provides the nosebleed-interest rate loan the driver arduously pays each month. Pace yourself, champ, and handle your liquor.

Is it rude to talk on my cell during a ride?

There is some basic information that needs to be confirmed at the beginning of a ride. Most importantly, who you are and if this is *your* ride. Don't enter the car talking on your cell and not acknowledge your driver. Drivers also need to make sure the address you input into your app is correct. I cannot tell you how many times I have confirmed the address, only to have the passenger apologize because they pushed the first default address that popped up on their screen. Stop chatting with your best friend long enough to greet your driver, and make sure you are delivered where you want to go.

Is it mandatory that I converse with my driver?

I have been asked many times if it is rude not to chit-chat with your driver. I don't think so. As previously mentioned, it is necessary to firm up the ride details. But after that, do what you want. It's your dime, your ride. Feeling optimistic and want to browse Tinder? Be my guest. You won't offend me if you don't want to talk. However, if you are in a mood for a conversation, I am more than willing to oblige. In fact, I would prefer it. There have been many interesting discussions in my car, and this book would not have been possible without those conversations.

LAST THOUGHTS

For most of us, rideshare use has become a part of our lives. So much so, the word *ubering* is often used as a verb, regardless of whether someone is using Uber or Lyft. Like Google ('Let me google it'), I have heard it said that when your corporate name is used as a verb, your company has arrived.

Despite the mainstream acceptance of fee-based rides, the future of the rideshare industry is uncertain. With the outbreak of Covid-19, restaurants and bars closed, rider safety concerns became a reality, and people became less enthusiastic about using Uber and Lyft. Combine these concerns with the fact that both are publicly-traded companies and have stockholders to appease, and the financial outlook of these public transport firms is, in the foreseeable future, questionable at best.

Here are a few highlights (or lowlights) from 2020:

• Uber's Ride Bookings were down 80% in April.

• No more pooled rides.

• Uber laid off 25% of its staff, Lyft 17%

All of this brings up a few interesting questions. What effect does a technological advancement like Uber have on our lives? How have these conveniences altered our lives, and as importantly, our habits? Additionally, what do we do if there is a disruption in the service, like we have now, and those habits have become a dependency?

I don't know about you, but once all the establishments open up again, I can't imagine losing the ability to request a safe ride home. It has become a consistency in my world, and likely in yours as well.

Rideshare was born from technology, and disrupted an entire industry. Now that our lives have improved because of the service, or at least made more convenient, what should we do if the benefit is no longer available, or we are not comfortable using it anymore? On the operator side of the equation, what would happen to all the drivers who depended on the income generated from this unique contractual position? If consumer demand decreased, and/or if safety concerns outweighed the flexible advantages of the job, millions of drivers around the globe would be displaced, creating a huge labor gap.

We live in a world of instant gratification, where the push of a button can get us almost anything we desire. These advancements provide benefits to the company, consumer and employee. But even if rideshare does get taken away, it likely won't be the last we see of it.

Recently, we have all had to make adjustments and compromises to our daily routines. Personally, I stopped driving because of this unforeseen pandemic, and am not comfortable resuming my driving, under any circumstances. It altered my behavior, changed my life, and forced me to pivot. Think about all the technology that makes your life easier. If Uber and Lyft were to stop operations, could you do without the service?

While I sincerely hope my stories provided some entertainment value, on a deeper level, I hope this behind-the-scenes look at the world of ridesharing caused you to become more empathic toward your drivers, and examine how technology has altered your life and theirs.

Gig drivers are lifesavers—literally and figuratively. They transport you to the airport and make sure you get to your business meeting on time. Show them your appreciation. If you give your stylist or a favorite barista a gratuity, do the same for your driver. Not only because they made sure you arrived safely, but because you likely weren't in any condition to operate a vehicle anyway. I always felt contented that in some small way, my driving contributed to the reduction of DUIs. I hope a life or two was saved in the process.

To all the passengers who kept me laughing and inspired me to pursue my literary dream, I thank you. The personalities and conversations of these wonderful people made the long hours bearable.

ACKNOWLEDGEMENTS

To my (not so little) monkeys, I cannot tell you how much you mean to me. You are an inspiration to me. Thanks for your encouragement when things were challenging, and for always making me laugh. Thanks for putting up with me when I was exhausted, and tolerating my gloomy moods. You alone gave me the strength to persevere, and helped me believe that hope, with conviction, makes all the difference. Thanks for being strong these last few years. I am very proud of you both, and love you more than know.

To my parents and family, who always provided unconditional love, the environment to try new things, and the foundational support that allowed me to pursue my goals. Thanks for enduring the undulations, as I have not always taken the easy path. Rest in peace Dad, hope you are proud of my work. I miss you very much.

To my dear friends: Ned, Bill & Judi, Russ & Robin, Mary & Deb, Yvonne & Gary, Jim, Ed, Issom, and the poker crew. Thanks for always believing in me, and motivating me when I stumbled. Thanks for your sage advice, listening to all my crazy ideas, and giving me a chance when others gave up.

To my wonderfully patient editor, Staci Frenes, of Grammar Boss Editing, https://www.grammarboss.com. Your guidance and expertise throughout this writing process was greatly appreciated. Thanks for taking my writing from a mad rant to a more reasonable presentation.

A special thanks to Shareen Rivera and her team at Rising Above Publishing Services, https://shareenriveacom.square.site/rising-above-publishing. You took my manuscript, worked your magic and made it shine.

To "Shawn Cody," who allowed me to develop the confidence and express myself creatively when this book was only an idea and a blog.

To my subscribers and online followers, thank you for all the support as I traveled down this unusual literary path.

To the millions of rideshare drivers who endure the countless miles and declining wages, my hat goes off to you, you have my ultimate respect. My sincere wish is that transporting others allows you a path to your dreams, or at the very least, a transition to your next adventure.

Finally, to the thousands of passengers from my driving days, thank you for inspiring me. You made me laugh, sing, cry, and frustrated the hell out of me at times. You enabled me to start a fitness business, motivated me to write a book, and allowed my "off the grid" survival for a while in Silicon Valley.

Portions of this book were featured in the Drivingfool blog, https://drivingfool.com, where I first shared my rideshare craziness with the world.

REFERENCES

Introduction

1. Melissa Berry, How Many Uber Drivers Are There? https://therideshareguy.com/how-many-uber-drivers-are-there/ (Aug. 10, 2020). (Page 5)

Sweet Music to My Ears

2. Brian Johnson, Angus Young, Malcolm Young. You Shook Me All Night Long. AC/DC. Atlantic, 1980, Album. (Page 10)

3. Ibid (Page 11)

Trouble with the Principal

4. Pinewood School, https://www.pinewood.edu/admissions/tuition (Page 14)

Muskrat Love

5. Neil Sedaka and Howard Greenfield. Love Will Keep Us Together, Captain and Tennille. A&M, 1975, Album. (Page 20)

6. Ibid. (Page 21)

7. Ibid. (Page 21)

8. Smokey Robinson and Ronald White. My Girl. The Temptations. Gordy, 1964, Album. (Page 22)

9. William Alan Ramsey. Muskrat Love. Captain and Tennille. A&M, 1976, Album. (Page 25)

Timing is Everything in Silicon Valley

10. Diane Ransom, The 'Do-or-Die' Moment That Led to Box's Billion-Dollar IPO, https://www.inc.com/magazine/202002/ diana-ransom/aaron-levie-box-ipo-public-sale.html/ (Winter 2019/2020 Issue of Inc. Magazine). (Page 36)

11. Ben Winck, Former Uber CEO Travis Kalanick has been cashing in shares since early November. Here's why his next sale may be his last, https://markets.businessinsider.com/news/ stocks/travis-kalanick-sells-72-million-uber-stock-dump-whole-stake-2019-12-1028783855#/ (Dec. 24, 2019). (Page 36)

12. Joseph Campbell and Phil Cousineau (preface), The Hero's Journey: Joseph and His Life and Work (Harper & Row, 1990). (Page 37)

Looking Over the Edge

13. Tom Wijman, The Global Games Market Will Generate $152.1 Billion in 2019 as the U.S. Overtakes China as the Biggest Market,https://newzoo.com/insights/articles/the-global-games-market-will-generate-152-1-billion-in-2019-as-the-u-s-overtakes-china-as-the-biggest-market/ (June 18, 2019). (Page 43)

14. The International Dota 2 Championships, https://www.dota2.com/international/overview/ (2019). (Page 43)

15. How to Make Money on Twitch (Ultimate Guide for Streamers), https://influencermarketinghub.com/make-money-on-twitch/ (Feb. 29th, 2020). (Page 44)

Is That Pepper Spray?

16. Dan Mangan, Suspect in Assault of Uber Driver Edward Caban Is Taco Bell Executive, https://www.nbcnews.com/news/us-news/suspect-assault-uber-driver-edward-caban-taco-bell-executive-n456361/ (Nov. 3, 2015). (Page 99)

In My Opinion

17. Andrew J. Hawkins, Uber is doing 70 percent fewer trips in cities hit hard by coronavirus, https://www.theverge.com/2020/3/19/21186865/uber-rides-decline-coronavirus-seattle-sf-la-nyc/ (March 19, 2020). (Page 153)

Why I Stopped Driving

18. Harry Campbell, Uber to Cut Rates in More than 100 Cities, https://therideshareguy.com/uber-to-cut-rates-in-more-than-100-cities/ (Jan. 8, 2016). (Page 155)

19. Graham Rapier, Uber's New Rates are Designed to Make Driver Payout More Consistent, But Some Say it Has Decreased Their Earnings, https://www.businessinsider.com/new-uber-pay-rates-hurt-earnings-drivers-say-2018-12/ (Dec. 3, 2018). (Page 155)

Last Thoughts

20. Faziz Siddiqui, Coronavirus is Forcing Uber to Return to its Start-up Roots, https://www.washingtonpost.com/technology/2020/05/26/uber-coronavirus-pivot/ (March 26, 2020). (Page 165)

REARVIEW MIRROR

*True Stories of Unusual Rides and Crazy Passengers
From a Late-Night Uber Driver*

BRIAN DIXON

"THE DRIVINGFOOL"

Made in the USA
Monee, IL
17 January 2021